FORTY-NINE STEPS

FORTY-NINE STEPS

FORTY-NINE STEPS
IN A
MALE MIDLIFE CRISIS

MORTEN MELDGAARD

Archway Publishing books may be ordered through booksellers or by contacting:

Archway Publishing
1663 Liberty Drive
Bloomington, IN 47403
www.archwaypublishing.com
1 (888) 242-5904

Because of the dynamic nature of the Internet, any web addresses or links contained in this book may have changed since publication and may no longer be valid. The views expressed in this work are solely those of the author and do not necessarily reflect the views of the publisher, and the publisher hereby disclaims any responsibility for them.

Any people depicted in stock imagery provided by Getty Images are models, and such images are being used for illustrative purposes only. Certain stock imagery © Getty Images.

ISBN: 978-1-4808-8954-5 (sc)
ISBN: 978-1-4808-8953-8 (hc)
ISBN: 978-1-4808-8955-2 (e)

Library of Congress Control Number: 2020906925

Print information available on the last page.

Archway Publishing rev. date: 07/07/2020

FORTY-NINE STEPS
Forty-Nine Steps in a Male Midlife Crisis

> The girl behind the counter has a tattooed tear on her left cheek
> One for each year he is away she said
> Nah, there is nothing wrong with her a hundred dollars won't fix.
> *Tom Waits*

This collection of essays and stories, poems and comments was written during a process of coming of age. They are neither fiction, biography, nor reflect a self-help manual. They are, to some extent, a weeding of the author's garden of consciousness but also ripples in our shared ocean of wisdom. As the Russian filmmaker Andrej Tarkovskij said in his book called *Sculpting in Time*, these stories are universal because they are singular, and every human shares exactly this quality, that they are unique expressions of life. The text is made up of three voices: a personal one, an analytical one, and a transcendent one. You could call them higher self, ego, and id. You could call them I am, small I, and prisoner. All according to your politics and inclination. But why call them anything? They are integral parts of the story, and as in life, each has a part to play.

This is not a religious book. Though all books may said to be religious since they point to a fragment of cosmic consciousness just by being there. Garden manuals, how to win influence and create friends, *The Satyricon*, I Ching—these all contribute to the collective body of knowledge, as do Batman, the Simpsons, and the colored pin-up books from the fifties. They use the same system of containing knowledge, and in this, they are sacred, whatever else they may convey. The Bible and a volume of the war speeches by Winston Churchill share this trait; they were lettered, printed, and bound, and then read by someone whose consciousness was deeply affected by what was read. It's a kind of magic we have. Printing books.

This book was written by a male someone growing up in a Marxist-Lutheran welfare society in northern Europe, devoid of any spiritual or religious dimension. Art was something they had at the local museum, and philosophy was something they taught in university. Religion was in church, and you only went there for Christmas. Since we didn't believe in Christ, we could have called it Xmas, but that was American, and in the seventies, the United States was off-limits too.

This background has proven to be quite a gift in later years when it occurred to me that other people have had bad experiences with religion. In my mind, religion is a system, a system just like the Metro. You need a ticket, and that ticket is your faith. Sometimes they also ask you to give up your better judgment, and this is where it gets tricky. In this book, I am referring to Christianity, which came part and parcel with the society I grew up in, and to Hinduism, which was a chance encounter. Buddhism and Taoism were families of choice and are, in my mind, techniques, like plumbing or printing are also techniques to obtain a given end. That end might be magical, as with printing books, or it might be practical, as with plumbing. Though the latter is more lethal than practical if you use lead for plumbing, like the Romans. So have a care. The medicine or earth wisdom portrayed in this book, I perceive as models. They can be manipulated to gain information, just like a diagram or computer model. The term "medicine" comes from a misunderstanding of Native American speech propagated by the early Europeans settling in North America. The term means whole and holy, thus pointing to a holistic vision of society only obtainable by using the cosmological model of the medicine wheel. This book contains a blending of many of these traditions with a certain focus in mind: to create hope.

So even if this is not a religious book or a spiritual self-help manual, the reader will find ample consideration and thought given to these matters. What is the difference in the status of emotion between a Buddhist and a Hinduist? Perhaps this is irrelevant when you find yourself in the Metro at 7 a.m., yelling at your soon-to-become teenage son and seeing the other adults thinking theirs. But when you reflect and try to change yourself and your attitude toward the emotion called anger, then this narrow, almost academic question gains huge importance. This notion of walking in circles, of posing the same question over and over through compulsive behavior is also echoed in the text. Sometimes it repeats itself, just like we do, until we learn. I learned that from Kafka. To make the text do what you want instead of just saying what you want. If you want to summon a labyrinth, don't just describe it in words; create a labyrinth of words.

This book was written as process. A satori. A cleansing. But it is also a coming of knowing, a coming to my senses. Perhaps it is the same genre as the self-delivery of the seventies where I grew up, but you will find very little information of whom I slept with, what I ate, or whom I dislike. This book is a mix, *mestizo*, between traditions, styles, genres, between singular and universal, between me and you.

This book testifies to one aspect of existence, namely, the reality of a so-called inner life. It is about creating, establishing, nurturing, and evolving an inner life as a basis of hope. It will have an occasional mentioning of what I drank, since the process of writing was also that of leaving serious self-medication. But the book is not about drinking; it is not therapeutic. It is about nurturing and maintaining a healthy relationship with yourself and your spirit. A rich inner life is cardinal to the well-being of any human, and this book is about that. In the humdrum of everyday life, e-mails, iPad policies, menopause, budget cuts, fake news, climate crisis, and what have you, this book is about hope. About building hope. Nurturing hope. Expressing hope. For what? That there might soon be a future where we all realize that love is the highest expression of knowledge, truth, and progress.

Lion Heart, Kvistgaard, September 2020

IN THREE SENTENCES

Be patient. Trust your nature. Change yourself.

GARDEN OF CONSCIOUSNESS

Pythagoras was not just anybody.
He taught us how to calculate the side of a triangle.
Triangulation, they call that now.

He taught us the harmony of the strings.

He held deep knowledge on how
To live your life
In harmony.

He said that there are seven life circles,
Each containing seven years.

These seven-year cycles make up our life experiences.
So at forty-nine, you arrive at either wisdom or despair.

Now, standing there at the terminal station,
You just might want to look back
At the spiral of your life.

Then remember that the first three cycles of the seven
Are the most formative.

In the first, you grow your instincts.
In the second, you grow your emotions.
In the third, you grow your logic.

So how can I live peacefully
If one of these circles is damaged?
That is why I must do my work.

In all these circles, many people have planted the seeds
Of their own beliefs and fears.
Those seeds are now growing in your consciousness.

So how can I live in peace
If one of these circles in my garden of consciousness is full of weed and misgrowth?
That is why I must do my work.

That is why I must become a gardener,
A gardener of my consciousness.

I REMEMBER

On the morning after, to see the pink dawn above the city and feeling deep in my heart that the sky was answering our prayer. The dream of a flowering earth, made real inside the Marble Church. To be inside the church, feeling the whole of the energy system change during the beautiful concerts, was to feel humble, to serve, to know love, to be fulfilled. But also, in other times, when I was looking at the beautiful Monet painting in Naoshima Island and knowing that we are all working on the same picture, singing the same song, hearing the song, being the song, singing the song. To know the strokes, admire them, love the painting, being it myself with my eyes, resonating with it.

My term for this experience of being utterly loved, totally in sync, outside and inside any subjectivity, humble, oneness, clarity, life force, effortlessly is the "Great-Grandmother." The big pink cloud of the Great-Grandmother outside time and space. Yes, there might be a Jehovah, a Christ, a Krishna, a Great Spirit. After all, there is creation. But outside, before this, there is the energy that I am remembering.

A friend of mine knows a great physicist working on the grand unified theory. His idea is that if the big bang is just an energy bump on *the way*, you can measure the depth of black holes. So I am thinking that *the way* is Tao, the literal translation of "the way," and as the Tao de Ching says, Before God was Tao, and she was complete. That all things are borne of woman. The experience of this is what I am remembering when I step into the first practice of the East.

I AM SINGING

During the last week, I have been singing my I am statement. It has become an I am song, and it is changing with me, getting flavor and color. It is sometimes melancholic, sometimes very poetic, sometimes very beautiful and joyful, and filled with light and love. There is a great softness come over me. Perhaps even a sorrow, at least an understanding of other people's needs, their turmoil, their hardships, and their dreams, hopes and longings. Sometimes I see myself from the outside. With great love and understanding, I see the vanity, even pretense, of my I am statement, and I feel with everybody trying to dance a dance that they don't know how to, to be what they have not yet become, to manifest what they can scarcely dream themselves yet. In this I have added a line to my I am statement:

> "He plunged in and swam about, and let the small jangling noise of his troubles be swallowed up by the innumerable laughter of the sea."
> "Eh?"
> "κυματων ανηριθμονγε λασμα—quotation from the classics. Some people say it means the dimpled surface of the waves in the sunlight- but how could Prometheus, bound upon his rock, have seen it? Surely it was the chuckle of the incoming tide among the stones that came up to his ears on the lonely peak where the vultures fretted at his heart."
> (Dorothy L Sayers, *The Man with No Face*)

So I am adding lines, and words. The I am melody is ever-changing. It's the jinglejangle of the Sweet Thursday. It's the good old jingleballicks. I feel good about it, feel playful. Full of sorrow. Feeling the poetry, the fragility, the breath of life, the song of life singing itself through me. Like a fat man ascending from a swimming pool, I am letting go of the serious "statement-ness" of my I am statement and just letting it be a song. A children's rhyme. Jingle-jangle. This is bringing me close to my humanness, my vulnerability, my humor.

GRANDFATHER FIRE

The fire blessing is something very sacred for me. I have a candle in front of my statue of the Holy Mary. I light it and say my prayer to her and to the grandfather, fire. I ask for a blessing to keep me through my day, a blessing to keep my inner fire intact and to keep me awake, affectionate, compassionate, alive, and filled with love and light, no matter what will arise during the day to dampen my spirit or quench the fire of my soul.

I have experienced that after I have started doing this prayer and asking for the fire blessing, the things encountering me and challenging me have taken absurd proportions. I will still be forced outside my center for a shorter or longer time, but the incidents that it takes to make me lose my grounding have reached a considerable size. More often than not, I simply sit down and laugh. I am laughing at the teaching. Is this what it takes to make me flip out? Sometimes it is the absurdity or the mere persistence.

I feel that when I collect myself in the midst of these "attacks" of bad-natured coincidence, I can let my affiliation with them go. If I succeed in letting go, of no longer relating, they either lose significance and, in some circumstances, they simply disappear or go into themselves again.

MEXICAN DIARY

Yucatan is pretty weird place. Running down the jungle on the freeway you can smell the corruption, the narcs, the excesses. And then the lushness of the jungle itself, the energy of the volcanic soil, the beauty of the Caribbean Sea.

We are living in a small modernist dream deep inside the jungle. The resort isn't really finished, so we got a bargain, which means that power and internet is driven by a generator. This isn't a problem since we are the only guests.

Today I was doing a small ceremony by our own private Cernottes. That's an open underground water deposit made by volcanic rock. The energy of it is terrific. You can almost talk to it. I sacrificed the tobacco from my small kiva prayer bundle in it. Kiva is the time of the four winter moons.

What came to me was that in order to stand within this kiva dream, I have to focus on one thing and forget the other. I have to focus on my relationship with my oldest son, how he mirrors me, and how I mirror him in disliking in him what I don't accept in myself.

So, this standing is about discipline that focuses on a single challenge and seeing this as *the* practice, the practice from which you practice all the others as well. If I can learn the practice of not entering the conflict but seeing the teaching, I can also see us both with respect in our own inner lights.

OVERLOOKING THE JUNGLE

I remember WindEagle taking us to the Mayan pyramid in Yucatan. Climbing it, we stopped midway to look out and realized that we climbed above the level of the forest. But that was in my mind, in the meditation that WindEagle taught me during one of our sessions of learning earth medicine and the directions of the wheel.

I have been doing that meditation ever since in the Southeast, going down into the temple, entering stillness, expanding to the universe, coming into oneness, and activating appreciation of this universe.

Today I am listening to WindEagle's deepening of this practice on my cell phone after concluding an excursion with my students here in Yucatan and climbing a pyramid, just like the one in the meditation. I realize that there is no meditation, no difference between mind and matter, only oneness and a multitude of reflections and refractions.

THE WARRIORS

I have been doing the Southeast wheel two or three times a week for many months as a part of doing the whole medicine wheel in my meditation. Usually, I would go to the ocean and rest in the sauna while doing the different wheels. After each wheel, I took a bath in the ocean and felt the embrace of the waves washing away all the energies that I collected during my work and stay inside the city. This is my mental, physical, and spiritual hygiene and the coldness and crispness of the Nordic nature are soothing together with the heat of the sauna. I sit there and watch the sun-speckled ocean or when heaven and sea are almost indivisible in the fog. It is my treasure, my sacred space, my most holy sanctuary. In the sun, whether it is four or twenty-four degrees Celsius, it is paradise to walk down the boardwalk knowing that I am of the stars, both walking here in the sunlight of our own star and walking freely among the stars and clouds of the galaxy.

As we arrive in Chichen Itza things get confused. They are about to close and we are late, because we have been waiting for the afternoon sun to show us the serpent coming down from heaven. But the great pyramid is not the only thing to see. As an architect it is a MUST to see the temple of warriors. Its what we came to see, from a professional point of view. Not the word become flesh, but the columns and platforms of sacred ORDER. I have to choose. Its cloudy, and the sun is not coming out. The guide wants us to go. The crowd is surly, thinking that the sun will set before the clouds open. I really need my still point. I need to feel the focus. To stay and hope for the opening that might not materialize or to go and see what I came for? I choose to stay. I am looking at the pyramid, as the clouds open and the crowd goes mad... everybody is fleeing to the base of the pyramid to see the spectacle. It is extravagant. It is an event. We miss out on the warriors.

THE JOURNEY IS OVER

I am practicing finding my still point in my hare chakra, directing my consciousness and energy there. To just let go and release myself in the great sea of tranquility. I just want to stay there. In the timeless, with the great-grandmother, the Tao. Then conscience return. The world. Space and time. This life and time. Me. What I am here to do. Feeling the deep teaching in letting the warrior go. Knowing that this incarnation is not about fighting, fighting the lost cause against evil to make an existence, to make a living, for the nation. The warrior needs to go. Or rather, to come back in a new guise.

I am reading Don Miguel Ruiz' *The Four Agreements*. To hold my word clean, not taking anything personally. Not presuming anything. Doing my best. Those rules. But first and foremost, holding clean my word. Not punishing, degrading, lying, manipulating, hurting. But using my word to create light and love around me. Unveiling the light and love that is immanent in all and everything by pointing to it with my word. Self-discipline of the warrior, as the discipline to listen to my heart, listen to my higher self while holding my small I am, appreciating the seeker-teacher relation.

I wake up at four in the morning. I am at home, in my bed. The journey is over. The kiva is over. I am resting in the quiet. Another journey will come. Another kiva will come. This is just the journey continuing. There is no end. I just stepped out of a dream and into a new dream. In this new dream, I feel life around me pulsating. My wife, my kids in the bed beside me, I am happy. I feel love. All the notes and all the sketches and wheels that I have been drawing in these last four moons come together as one wheel with eight points. What I need to do. What priorities I need to make. It's like a shopping list. That concise. But also filled with promise. With love.

EIKOS

I am aware that I am feeling worried about economic concerns. That I am too lavish with my spending. I feel deep down that there is endless flow, that this is not a money incarnation. But I need to focus on being more exact. That economy comes from Eikos, meaning household. That the boundless resource that I am feeling is on the other side of the river of holding house. I appreciate the teaching. I embrace it. Remarking how the fear, the feeling, the knowledge, the intuition come into one sureness. Knowing that the knot in my stomach is not there to stay, just nudging me, urging me to make some things clear. To manifest them. Practice them. By holding my own house.

I focus on my private economy. On the economy of the school. Both the travel and the staff economies. Then on my house. We are redoing the foundation. It's taking forever. The grandfather stones coming up the basement are making me nervous. Should I have let them rest? What about the cost? They can only cast a meter at a time of this new foundation. I remember laughing at this and sharing at the Northwest ceremony, then the process came to a halt. We couldn't move. Now we are actually doing it, creating a new foundation. It's paradoxical while I am doing this deepening journey. But they know what they are doing. I could not have found better people to do this work. It's like being keyed up for an operation. You know you need to do it, but there it is. It's unnerving. That's okay. I will hold that.

THE GIRL FROM THE
RAINBOW FACTORY

I am awake. It's two a clock in the morning. So is my daughter, Vega. Star Eagle is making rainbows in her coloring book. We have jetlag. Woke up an hour ago. No more sleep. Tomorrow I have the day off—and many more days—to concentrate on my process. Fall is my busy time. That has ended. I planned this. Myself. I am loose. This semester I will mostly have to plan for the coming fall. I am vacant. Then why do I feel guilty? Because we should be in bed now? Because I am privileged? God knows, I worked like an animal right up to our Mexico trip. Because I still have some knots to tie? I tell myself that I love and forgive myself. That I choose to love and forgive myself even though I feel guilty for God knows what, being alive? I go beyond the boundary.

I used to go into the temple. I would walk down the flagstone path, seeing the pyramid in the distance. Sometimes I would see Krishna and Radhi in the jungle and stop to talk to them. They hold great advice for somebody like me.

Then I would go to and ascend the ancient Mayan structure. Halfway up, I would pause, thinking on WindEagle, look out over the jungle, and realize how far I had already climbed. Right now, at this time of the morning, it seems like a dream that I actually did that. Went there in a physical waking dream. Climbing above the roof of the jungle. In the meditation, I climb the pyramid, I go down the stairs to the obsidian mirror; I look into it and see the whole of Yucatan, Mexico, the Earth Mother. Then the sun, the stars, our galaxy, and the other systems. There I rest.

In the waking dream, I was not alone. Like now, in the middle of the night in the rainbow factory, I was with StarEagle. That's her name, Vega. It comes from Arab, meaning both star and eagle. Like Siegfried, she already has a medicine name, the victorious peace. On top of the pyramid there was a small stone, like an ancient alter in front of a closed structure. Vega was sitting there as if she had never moved. Had she been there before? Was she returning or coming into her own? In the waking dream, the pyramid was steep, like a mountain. No railing and the stone slippery from use. As I am lying on the couch, StarEagle places a pink piece of volcanic glass on my stomach. I got that at the moon temple in Teotichuan. It has a deep healing vibration. Together with WindEagle's soothing voice, I find the still point beyond time, beyond thought.

PROFOUND OPENNESS

I am into a rhythm now, doing my daily practice. Profound openness helps me to see deeper. I have gone into the economic concerns and differentiated them. The most important one is the one about the economy of our family. My concern is that kids are expensive, and over the years, I have been injecting a lot of money in our monthly budget. While discussing this, my wife says that she has actually started to make some money and that she would like to make this contribution in the future. Now I don't feel nervous anymore. I don't feel alone with my worry. I feel that I am in a relationship that holds me and that we are together in maneuvering the boat. I am open to this. I accept the teaching and the feelings of concern as guides showing me how our relationship can deepen.

Going through the numbers, we realize that our eldest son, has been taking out a lot of money to buy assets in an online game that he is playing. I guess we thought that only happened to other people. It's not really the Skyhorse ticket at all. He actually found the code in Mom's notebook and bought all this virtual crap on the internet. Wauv. How do you stay profoundly open to something like this? We make a ceremony where he has to give back the money—in cash—to understand the reality and consequence. It's like all the money he ever saved. Then we ask him a simple question: "Why are you here? Come back when you can answer that, and we'll turn on the Internet again."

GROWING EDGE

How can I value my growing edge? I am uptight with my two boys. My intuition tells me it has something to do with the will space. In my yoga, it is the place of enjoyment. It is controlled by guilt. Working with this place makes a lot of old issues come back. I am feeling very acutely that I need to let my youngest son out of my energy system and that when I can stand in my own force, I'll also help My oldest by setting an example. I feel this has a lot to do with my father. He had a strong will and imposed this on me. I never understood why he would do that. I loved him, but I didn't understand why his answer to this was to control me. Now I am doing the same thing when I am not in my I am, while trying in my growing edge to release my sons from this pattern. It's not that easy to navigate. Or appreciate. Perhaps I can see them both as my teachers, helping me to let go of the past while appreciating the teaching. Valuing that they are earning their own experiences and making room for them to harvest that.

In my experience I wouldn't have minded if my father had let down his facade and said, "Okay, this is what I tried to teach you. Now you are grown up. How do you feel about it?" He taught me never to give up, which is valuable; I value that. But it also comes with the price of not being able to quit. Having to presume, continue, press on. Perhaps I just need to learn to quit. Perhaps I already know; I just have to open up for it.

If I define the growing edge as something I don't know how to, I define it negatively. It becomes an assignment in class. A difficult piece of math that I have to do before I can go out to play. It's a form of self-hate, of punishment. I need to do the assignment because I am not good enough, not perfect already. If I was perfect, I wouldn't have to grow. What kind of thought is that? Where did that come from? Perfect things grow, and they grow slowly. That's why we have a growing edge. That's why the trees have orerings. Why? Well, because they are perfect.

I AM

I am a cascade of starlight.
I am light manifest as matter.
I am white light from the mouth of infinity returning.

I am the clear spring, the eternal well, and again, a sacred spring.
I am the one who returns.

I am the lion heart
I am the lovers in the field,
I am the broken arrow and the sheated sword

I am the flowering of the golden tree.
I am the knowing smile on the lips of the holy mother.
I am the flower of the elders' dreaming.

I am shadows of the grass and the leaves singing.
I am the innumerable laughter of the sunlit waves at sea.

I am the table, laid ready in the wilderness
and the bride stripped naked by her bachelors
even this worldly vessel on my spirit journey.

I am in this life with gratitude and servitude.
I am in these lives as the green fire of spring.
I am in the womb of the holy mother as the light behind darkness.
I am in the pink cloud with the great-grandmother outside time and
space.

HUMAN CONSCIOUSNESS

The nature of humanity is to be the consciousness of Mother Earth.

But what is nature?
What is it to be a human?
What is consciousness?
What is Mother Earth?

In the beginning, humans were one with Mother Earth. With the advent of human consciousness and ability to reflect intellectually on our existence, we became separated from our origins and each other. Our destiny lies in once again realizing that we are one with Mother Nature in order to become the reflecting consciousness of the earth. That is what we are.

BUCKY

Buckminster Fuller taught us that we live on spaceship earth. So, we are all astronauts, and Mother Earth is our spaceship. But the moment is also a vessel. This eternal moment is also a ship. This fleeing moment is eternally rolling through history, like a ship voyaging on the vast ocean of time. It may seem that we are leaving known shores behind and that green ones await us behind the silver curtain, but this is only the illusion of the traveler. We are all on the same journey, together in the same eternal moment.

IN ANOTHER THREE SENTENCES

I am trusting the process. Everything is as it should be. I can't do anything wrong.

MOTHER NATURE
_clearing out her deadwood

Mother Nature is clearing out her deadwood. That's what came to me this morning. That is what I need to do. That is who I want to be. Who I wanna work for. To quit working for the human social dependency system and start working for Mother Nature.

Mother Nature's son. Isn't there a Lennon-McCartney song that goes like that? I always found Paul too much of the mother-in-law's dream. The pretty boy, and now here I am at it. From the *White Album,* but no judging.

That album was nice though. Great inspiration, room for all the different voices inside. Got that when I was fourteen. What was my state then? The last days I have been feeling like I could go in and out of my past like doors in a vast empty mansion. The Whitey album, Sonic Youth; I wonder, *When was that?*

I remember being in the car with my dad and getting the Sister album on a cassette deck from Bule, my new friend. My first real friend since childhood. Seeing them live the week before, Thurston Moore thrashing ever so many guitars and piling them in a freight case. But just opening that door, going into the feeling of having a new friend, a real friend. How I loved him. Being with him. Hanging out. Staying out. Going downtown. Sitting with his dad in the big house. Drinking red wine till late in the night. "The Castle" we would call it. And we would call his dad "the old guy" after the German detective series *Der Alte.* In the beginning, he smoked. Camels, I remember. I didn't smoke myself. Not yet. Arne, that was his name, would come into the squat to see his sons play punk-rock gigs, enjoying watching the girls and being with young people. I liked that. He was just there. It was okay. Very different from my own dad. Not in a bad way. Just different.

My mom and dad. They had just divorced. I hear the clicking of a truck parking, and the guys downstairs in the basement breaking up the foundations. We need a new foundation. The house is dead-right smack in the middle of the city. So it figures. They will have catering trucks pulling up the street at six in the morning, with me trying to write my morning pages. Clearing out the deadwood, and the guys downstairs trying to get to work and do the basement before morning traffic begins.

I was at the stone in Lalita, Spain, when I did the meditation on the house. Could I live inside town again? We had spent some eight or nine years in a suburb and needed to leave real bad. Partly because of the people we were with, partly because we needed the change. I am trying to be fair. It was a nice place, after-all. It was the childhood place of my two boys. I remember going to the nearby forest. Playing our own invented game, Roller golf. Me drinking beer at the lake, feeding ducks, and then vodka and juice in a small filler.

At Lalita, I went out in the hills at night, groping in the dark, old, overgrown fields or what used to be. All brambles and filter. But in the end, I found my way. I usually do. Standing on the big boulder by the river gorge it came to me: Be patient, trust your nature, change yourself. So I am. So I do. I felt that going inside town again would not let me rest in nature as I wanted but rather, let me see a bigger part of the globe, working with many people from across the globe. The blue house, or the green house as Vega would call it, because on top of the blue, it actually is green when the evergreen holds the upper hand. Vega is only four. She notices things. She sees. Everything depends on the eyes that see. I saw that. Chose it. For myself. Now I am holding another dream. The small thatched cottage, the horses, the trees. Peace. Writing. No more emails. That's what I am approaching with this text. Another livelihood. To move out of the city and into my own. That's the dream. I am dreaming it. Now.

I have arrived at dusk, the trip has made me dizzy. Remember arriving at Hydra Island in a cold and clammy beginning of March, already drunk from sipping scotch off a small plastic in the speedboat over—and returning full of apologies and regret, not really sure what happened. Buying avocado and vegetable juice, going on a detox, and starting paternal leave with Vega; each day going down to the supermarket determined not to buy any alcohol. Old friend, buried in ceremonial ground now. Remembering going out to greet him, just to make sure he was still in the ground every solstice and equinox. And then yesterday, at the ocean, only having finished the first wheel of the East and receiving the swan medicine. Your transformation has been concluded; you have been fulfilled. It is complete.

Discipline is hard these days. So is finding the rhythm together. Just keeping my pace. Keeping my peace. In the living room in front of me My daughter is crying, while her mother is lying on the couch. I need to write my morning pages. She is angry. The boys upstairs are watching telly, and she wants to be in on it. She is adamant. In this family, I am supposed to do something about it. Police it somehow. But I want to do my morning pages. I want to do my yoga. If I don't hold my inner peace, I'm not really much of a help to anyone.

That's how it is these days. Walking in beauty. I am starting with beauty in my words. Keeping my word clean. That's not easy with a little girl screaming at you, and a truckload of e-mails coming into your mailbox every day. But that's where I am at right now. Trying to walk the beauty way. Trying to do my morning pages. Doing my daily routine. Doing my yoga. Drinking my tea. Eating my vegetables. Walking with beauty around me. In front of me. Above me. In my footsteps. Walking with beauty in my thoughts. In my words. And in my actions. It took me a while to figure out why it didn't say anything about emotion. Beautiful emotion. Because those are neither bad or good. They are messages. They are energy. They can turn into beauty, or they can turn into something nasty. Depending on you. What your condition is. Your field-condition will determine if you react or respond. Like in responsible. For your emotions. For your life.

Morning pages. I am trying to do them. To clear out the deadwood. To become a clear channel. Yesterday I had a great sensation. Though. I was doing my yoga practice after a long spell of not doing practice. All week I had been uptight regarding budget cuts. Economic challenges in general, in all aspects of the wheel. At home, with the building project, the Mexico travel, and the BA-program that I am heading. I must admit I was blaming others, but the fact is, I spent too much on the Mexico travel, and I calculated an error. I was creating drama. I was blaming others. I was identifying with the situation. A = A.

Then I did my yoga. I realized the simplest answer to the equation. I had been making the old mistake. Taking the initial givens for granted, accepting how things had been laid out by others. But this is not the real learning. The real learning is how everything shifted like a lens-shift or through a kaleidoscope. Suddenly, everything was at peace, and I saw that the only one creating disharmony was myself. My own feeling of not being good enough, my own fear. Deep learning. Because this shift must be possible on a much larger scale. To let the veil of reality fall and see that everything is made of light and that love is the only reality.

Hard to realize Monday morning, feeling like an old worn-out warhorse. Four meetings to go. Then another day with three more all-day meetings. Then I can get away. Excuse me, but that is how I think. How can I escape? How can I unplug? When is it time for me to shake off the sawdust? No more workhouse blues. I realize that I must make the change where I am. I realize the calling. To send out five hundred students rounded by the medicine. But why five hundred? Why not settle for less? I miss the countryside. I miss nature. I look up in the air and I see the 5G antenna right across the street from where we live. I know that's not healthy. Neither is stress. All those e-mails. All that phone. I don't want a phone. I don't want e-mails. I want a landline. And real letters. If anyone cared enough to write. I remember the meditation by the stone. Trust your nature. Have patience. Change yourself. The nature inside me. Inside all of this. Trust that. Your inner nature. Be patient. Use the force of all this to change yourself. Become a monk in all this.

Tuesday. Still I didn't manage. I honor the agreement. The agreement of the blue house. I trust my nature. I am patient. I change myself. But it is hard for me. I am so afraid to step outside the security that this job I am in offers me. Knowing that it won´t be all peace and quiet and meditation on the other side. Still feeling deep inside how this is draining me that I am a coward. Not yellow but chicken. How I long for peace and quiet. Long for nature. For soothing and healing. I realize that I am building a foundation by going through this rough economic wakening. By writing these morning pages. Trying to catch up with the discipline of it. Not making the three pages a day. Not making the yoga practice. But trying. Hanging on. Until the bear awakens. Now it will be Easter soon. I made it so far. I can make it till the end of the week. Just have to get through to that, and then maybe I can skip coffee and get back on track. Think about that. Having trouble over coffee. Me—who skipped forty smokes a day and two six-packs—having trouble over coffee?

But that is how it is. Is affects my system. I become vulnerable. And then the energy system here isn't all that nice. They used to kill people here. Then it gets you down. As long as I am connected. Linked, chained to the spirit world. Re-legioned. Situated. It doesn't matter. I can stomach the teaching. But when I come down from that, I suffer. That's what it is. Suffering. In vain. Or realizing the agony of everyone. The failure. Of everyone. Of every hope. Of every good will. The utter and complete futility. Everyone thinking they are delivering words of flowers, finding out they only have thorns in their mouths. Ashes. Slags. Slugs. Knowing this pain of the spirit impotent in the flesh, longing but unable to arrive, to permeate the flesh and become present.

Only there as a shadow. A ghost. A twin. A doppelgänger. Feeling abandoned. Alone.

But God hasn't left us. Conscience will return. When it returns. That is what the medicine is in my life right now. The promise. The experience. The gift of a new day. A new hope. Another chance.

Knowing I was never alone. That I am not alone now. Only enjoying the privilege of experiencing how it feels to feel abandoned. Alone. Left by God. A delicacy perhaps. Dark delight. Kali Yuga. Whatever you may call it. Down here in the well of flesh. Heaved from the well of darkness. If everything is made from light, and love is the only reality, then darkness is matter. Slow light forming the known world and its boundaries. Earth.

This morning—Easter—I am starting with tea. The energy has shifted. Is shifting. I am shifting. Trying not to go into a quarrel with my youngest son about walking the dog. With my eldest about not watching media. I guess he is while I am writing this. I guess I am sitting here by the computer. Watching media. I am looking into the Easter time. Really needing to relax. To find peace and quiet. Not yelling at the kids. Especially Morgan, my oldest.

During my meditation at sea, my eldest has been holding a prominent space. As the teacher. As my teacher. Teaching me to become the teacher. It sounds funny perhaps. But after all this time, my son is the only one who can really get my goat. With his self-pity. With his blatant materialism. With his sole interest in what the others think of him. Of me. Of our family. I guess I am to blame, but where will that lead me? So I have decided that he is my teacher. In embracing difference. In understanding the other. In not choosing conflict. In stepping into my light incarnation. In consoling, in resolving, in being friendly, understanding, encompassing, loving. And he is a harsh teacher. I am not over the hill yet. I haven't broken the code. But now I am trying to build myself up again. With yoga. With tea.

In my other meditation. I see myself in the center. With the yoga. With the tea. With the medicine. Holding the dream of living in the country with the horses and the medicine. That dream is materializing by writing this. And by understanding the other wheel, my wife's wheel. Seeing how much she has on her plate. Understanding that she needs help in order not to fall. Seeing deep. How healing must come through her dad. Clearing up the mess. Then her mum. Then perhaps the past. What I need to do is to help her. Hold her. Then we have the children. Yes, my eldest son is my teacher, but they are also each to their own important people of the coming world. I need to teach them what they came here to know. Morgan about the medicine. Elias the yoga. Vega the Tai chi. Then comes the academy. As number four. Stop identifying with this job. See it for what it is. The students are there. That is what matters. Not all the stuff that I can't change. Not all the bad energy. Or the employees. The teachers. The institute wars. Forget about that. They are not yours. They are not you. You are the purple diamond. You are Vega coming to rest on your lap. You are the confidence of Elias's embrace.

Easter has started in my heart. The love of Jesus Christ runs very innocently through my veins. I remember in the bad days, when I was drinking a lot and didn't know what to do, I would go to the church of our Lady and pray and meditate in front of the statue of Christ. I also remember the Metope ceremony in June two years ago, when we started to pick weeds from our garden of consciousness. One of them being feeling alone. Not worthy to care about. But one of them actually turned out to be a gift. Growing up in a society totally devoid of religious, spiritual, or philosophical outlook. The Marxist-Lutheran materialist society. In retrospect, it has made me open to all sorts of religious and spiritual experiences. I actually get a lot out of saying the Mahatma mantra of the Hare Krishna, and it is the big mantra. Yes, it is. The biggest. If it makes any sense to compare mantras, but I guess if you can sell them for large donations, it does to some. So why is the best for free? Well, why is love free? The irritating thing is actually that you can't buy it. Rent it perhaps, lease it, but not own it, unless you own it yourself. Owning love. For yourself.

I think that is the concern of this Easter for me. How do I own my love for myself? It's not about others. It's not about intimacy, work, or sex. But simply about this: How do I own the love I have for myself?

I am seeing that I need to learn to keep my word clean. And that I need to help my wife carry her load. Yesterday I failed in both. I think. While listening to WindEagles's sermon on the South wheel. Being in between the raindrops. Readying my stance. Being tolerant. Reaching for wholeness.

And then blackout.

I am sitting here quietly. Watching the daffodils on the table that have come out during the night. I have the time for my own. I am drinking my holy basil tea. I can meditate. Write. Go to the ocean. I have the time and the scope. The two yellow candles that Vega and I bought are lit beside me. The energy of the sweet Lord is here with me. The statue of his mother that I bought after a drinking spell is here, and the sage is burning. So I am in the right place. In the blue house that Krishna picked for me. Everything is as it should be this Easter Sunday.

But I feel guilty. For getting into a quarrel with my wife. Well, I guess honestly that she started it. For taking the conflict with her on the phone my son wanted to bring. Well, he shouldn't. So perhaps I was right? WindEagle speaks about reaching for wholeness, to go beyond being right. How do you do that when the ones you are with or yourself are stuck in this? By listening to all the voices. By giving time to listen to your own inner voice. What does it say? Yesterday it said, *Why am I alone trying to do something?* It says that a lot. And some of it is right. Why am I alone? Why haven't I left? Because I am not really alone. The sweet Jesus is with me. And perhaps I am just a little ahead, not alone. But I feel that. In the intimacy, with the sensuality. I feel alone there. With the medicine for the family. For choosing the family. For trying. I am sensing that Veronica is just barely hanging on. That her artistic life is taking all that she has. And I feel that what I have to give, like the Cherish project, could only have been delivered with her. Not someone like her, but her. So is that it? No, there is more. It is only the beginning. I have to reach out for wholeness. Showing the others how it is done.

I'll go for a walk with Freddie, our dog, now and then do my morning practice. We also need to figure out where to put the medicine on the street. The boulders from downstairs need distribution all along the street, from canal to canal. I am also alone in this. But I don't feel it. I feel that I am five years old, playing, and that all the spirits are out there to watch me doing the medicine.

This morning is a late morning. I got up at eight thirty. It was a terrible mistake, so I slept on till eleven o'clock. Now the sun is out, and everything has this magical hue, like when I was a kid and saw pictures from the United States. It seemed that everything was made of cedar wood or pine and that everything was shining bright, and everybody was in love. With their kids, their spouses, the world. Those images also on the Sister album, a small boy walking in the grass on the lawn long ago.

The bright images of childhood. Right now, the electrician is here. My daughter is sitting, watching as he repositions our new designer lamp. Well new, PH designed that in the late twenties. But her memory of this house, of this time, this light. The daffodils flaming on the table in the red enameled pitcher. Freddie on the baroque sofa. Is this a good life? Is this a good childhood? Mom is standing in her overcoat, the electrician finishing and perfecting the hanging of the lamp. We have been waiting two months for him, and now he is here. He fixed it.

Emotional intelligence. This Easter it seems is a lot about gearing down. Letting the nervous system cool down. There has been a lot. Then I don't have to teach anymore. Only to steer the boat. If I can stop identifying with the academy, I might be able to step into the light. Well, I know I have to quit fully, but this is a start. Relaxing, breathing, realizing that everything is as it should be; everything is at peace, in balance, at rest, in order, just as it was meant to be. Perfect in itself. Whole.

I woke up this morning with an echo of something Veronica said yesterday. About being very feminine but putting on a shell of masculinity to fit in. I feel that this resonates about myself. I am that. Yes, there is the warrior, but in reality, there is spring, clear spring. In reality, there is a blending of feminine and masculine, and the hard shell I am presenting to the world is a fake. I am the spring. A female incarnation. Sacred spring. Like the drawing of my energy self I did at Lalita.

I was thinking about my friend the other day. He is so much yin. So soft. Bendable. But whenever he tries to talk about the outsides, he turns into a bigot. *Why do that at all?* I wonder. And when it comes to myself, *Why put on that hard shell?* Bite my teeth. The warrior is there as a shadow behind me. No one will come to plunder me. Why not be open, soft, loveable? And why not let the wise woman do all the economics, the worry that the warrior just gets mixed up about?

As I was thinking this, my wife was telling me that she is questioning why she works so much. I told her that she is between samurai and master, and she needs to let herself and her discipline go in order to go to the next level. Like Sifu and master Ugay in *Kung-fu Panda*. Seeing that everything is already complete. Keep on singing when your mouth is shut. I congratulated her that she has come so far into this to actually want to spend more time with her family. I love that. I support that. But I also support the clouds. The pink cloud. I also support her manifesting the sacred energy. Opening up to the sky field.

I am expanding this second. Like the space between the raindrops. Morning practices. Morning pages. I was meditating yesterday on embracing my feminine side. It felt very much like coming home. In the South I was laughing as the expression of the full potential was that my wife and I would be the two happiest lesbians in the world. If we can open up to that. I was reviewing the practices. Remembering to fill my body with light during the day in order to keep standing for the light. I'm looking at the pink and the purple diamond of volcanic glass that I bought in Mexico. So pretty they are. And filled with deep secrets.

I wake up with a soft hand on my cheek. I need that. My eldest has come home, and though the trip in the car down from the country was nice, he and his kid brother ended up in their usual conflict. And I joined them. I'm wondering why I am so angry. I'm thinking it has to do with our sexual life. I am not satisfied. In two months, we have slept together twice. That's not really enough for me. I don't know what to do. We did the tantra thing, and it helped a lot. But still, we are a long way apart. Right now, I am angry. I know why. My wife told me she was praying for different things. I think she should pray for us having a sex life.

Well, I guess you can't tell people what to pray for. But there it is. For me this is the sole thing ruining my life. Okay, I can zoom out and see the teaching in the situation with my eldest. I can see my own mistake. But in this, I am just suffering. I am trying. Holding the high dream. Praying. Doing courses. Talking. And still I am unsatisfied. It's not that I am dreaming of somebody else. I am dreaming of intimacy. Of sensuality. Lust. Why can't it be like that? I am wondering what is wrong. I don't know. I can't elevate the situation and see the teaching. What am I supposed to learn? To leave because I am unhappy? To set my demands? To accept the situation? To harvest the fruits of a very restrained sex life? What?

I am in the darkness here. I just don't know. And when I ask Veronica, she doesn't know either. Or she is lying. Or she thinks it is okay. Well, not okay. Just so-so.

So what am I praying for? What is the high dream? Well, the high dream is to live in love and life with my woman. To be joined in a spiritual, emotional, physical, working relationship and to be united in creating a family where love and light runs through us all. To have a deep sensual relationship with the woman in my life. To feel trust, love, intimacy, relationship, nearness, softness, tenderness. To feel held. Trusted. Loved. To be passionate. To forget everything else. To be united.

Okay, that didn't pan out. Instead, I am a menace. To my whole family. The boys have been doing Easter breakfast, and I am angry. I even start an argument with my wife, and the boys run around the house as poisoned mice. My youngest son starts playing the piano because he thinks he might get to play on his iPad. But when my eldest says that he would also like that, they get into a fight, and I get really mad. Great family. Happy Easter. And tomorrow. Well, there is no tomorrow because I am leaving on a course with my pathfinder.

What we are discussing is why we don't have a sex life like other people our age. Two or three times a week. We have sex once a fortnight—if that. I don't know why that is. Is my penis to small? Do I smell? Am I not the right type? Do I do the wrong moves? Or is there too little time? Are we too stressed? Is everything ending up in kids and work and work and kids? Okay, so we could scope out some adult time, but who should do that? Me, I guess.

So why is it that I am the only proactive adult around here? Why is that my job? Why am I alone in everything I do? At home? In my relationship? At work? Well, this is my anger and my self-pity speaking. And from this place, I ruin the only nice moment in Easter so far so that blame and self-hate can join the chorus. But what is behind all this? Okay, there is the theme of being alone, but I know that. I chose to come down here early. I chose to be the first. I chose to be alone. I am alone, and then I am not really alone because I know God is with me.

But God, whichever one of them you pick, wouldn't like me to terrorize my kids because I am not getting laid. So what is it that I have to learn here? What is the teaching?

That I hurt myself when I am hurting others. And then what?

It's Easter morning, and I wake up with the feeling of being wrapped in the energy of the pink image of Christ that I saw in Venice three years ago. Inside the Palazzo Cini, in the high-ceilinged galleries it was hanging. It even had an engraved heart in the paint. I remember the little plaza where my old boss would drink white wine while I was having sparkling water. It was a test. It was my Golgatha. To go on an outing with him, staying sober the whole time. But I made it. It was an ordeal. Going up to Veneto to film at the Carlo Scarpa cemetery. He was angry that I didn't want to drink, but I held my ground. That was like going through a boxing match. To this day, I can't believe I made it.

I am at Magic Moon Wolf's house. Yesterday we were doing a lot of meditations using crystals. I was meditating on my anger. How to understand it. How to make room for it. The warrior needs his anger to protect the sacred space, according to Magic Moon Wolf. In the first meditation, I saw that I need to embrace my wife as she is. I also saw the link between being unsatisfied and short tempered with my eldest, and I saw that I need to embrace him as he is. My son is or is not a chief; he will have to find out himself. Why is he here? What does he want? What did he come here to do? I need to keep my word clean. Using humor to do it, like a game. Oh, you got me there. Now I am angry and have to do the loser's dance. Flush. Then I need to turn the question of what are you here to teach me around. The question is, what did you come here to learn?

This morning it feels like the old wounds have been cleaned up. Venice also had a double dip, where I didn't make it. I wonder if I will go back to Venice at all. This Easter was like that. Not that my anger is wrong. But things have improved. I could talk to my wife about my feelings or ask her why she doesn't feel like having intimacy. It feels like the old pattern of being a victim of feeling alone has come in for its last bow. Well, not last; it is a part of me. But I guess I am reasoning like this. When I am taking on the burden of the kids, then I would at least like some intimacy. It's not like that. My eldest is my teacher, teaching me to hold my word clean. To find my humor. To stay in my center, no matter what. Like the tumbler in *Kung fu Panda*. He will test my center regardless. And my wife. Well, I don't have the right to make her go deep into herself. I can talk to her. I can engage her. We can do stuff together. But I can't force her. If she is happy as she is, then that's that. I have made my choice to be with her. I can change myself, but I have to accept her as she is. Well, I have to accept me as I am instead of being in the victim or the perfectionist all the time, creating drama.

Okay, so a couple of days when I haven't done my morning pages. Or yoga. Two days to be exact. Back at work. Lots of e-mails and stress trying to push me out of the center. This morning in the car I was pondering on emotional intelligence while listening to a podcast. I need that. Really deep. Instead of changing, we have to grow out of our difficulties. What is the difference here? That change creates the polarity of before and after, while growing is a continuous movement, bridging the old and the new, bridging what has to change with the change needed. We need to grow a new culture. Grow into a new culture. Not change. That's like Münchausen. Changing. Pulling yourself up by the hair. What good did change ever do for us? Growing is the potential for real change.

Then there is my own growing edge. Once again, getting out of the house became a contest between me and My eldest. I feel alone with the chores, remembering how great it was to have Yasouyo there. Alone with the lunch packs, alone with the dog, alone with starting up. I would like to start at four thirty, write, meditate, do morning practice, but something is stopping me. There is something to learn. I think it is this: I need to embrace my feeling of being alone. After all, I decided to come down to early. Come as one of the first. My own decision. So I am not alone. I am just one of the first. I am not alone. I am at the center of new growth. So how do I resonate with growing? With my growing edge? I am at the center. I have the best job in the world. The most wonderful woman. The most beloved kids. The best house. Or is it the other way around? That I am still a victim?

I was attending WindEagle's teaching fire yesterday on the internet. She was reading a piece by a young Norwegian poet, calling for a quiet revolution of love, of radical self-appreciating, of doing away with all the skepticism, self-hate, neglect, expectation, self-punishment. I felt that go directly to my heart as a ray of light hitting my body, going inside it, filling it up, exploding.

This morning we stayed in bed. Talking. This time I wasn't angry but explained to her that I really need the intimacy, the cuddling, the caress, the feeling of attraction, the desire, the sensuality, the sex in my life. Every day. I think she understood it this time. That it's not about sex. It's about feeling safe. Feeling wanted. Feeling attractive. Loved. Feeling respected. Feeling that my status as a man has substance. Here is a beautiful woman, and she loves me. It's about all these things. Not that my self-worth or self-esteem is dependent on her, but as she is in my life, I would like that life to be full and not frigid. For me, only then comes the humor and the play, then comes the surplus to go out and do fun stuff together, and then comes the strength to go through all my chores. Yazmin, our counselor, told me there were five kinds of love: gifts, words, touch, favors, time. I think I am the touching kind, and I guess Veronica is the favoring kind. So I have done a lot to help her with what she wants. Not because I want anything in return, but because I love her. Perhaps it is just hard to understand when you really want to change the world, that somebody else's most burning desire could be to have a sensual relationship with his wife. This is asymmetrical, perhaps, but then my most burning desire is to realize myself, and I am doing this with my fullest attention and energy.

New bundle. May has almost come. I am still trying to get up each morning, write my morning pages, do morning practice, do yoga. But it's not working. Perhaps there is more down here in the flesh world that I have left uncovered. My head is aching too. During the day I get more and more fresh, but at four thirty, I am not there. I did all of December, January, and February getting up at five. And now the energy has gone. The discipline. I am feeling sloppy. Not there at all. I have my yoga mat here. I could do my yoga right here in the office as soon as I am done writing. Then I won't have time to do the other stuff, but I will feel better.

The tea is out there in the kitchen. I will have to go and get that. I missed morning practice again. Both the traditional one and the yoga one. Today I have to do South medicine with the students. That won't do without morning practice. I will get the tea. Meditate a little. It's only eight o clock. There is plenty of time.

I find my still point. Watch each thought rising from the bottom like bubbles of air rising from a lake. I am at the calm center. I can go outside. Make the twenty count. I can sit here, meditating. There is plenty of time. Time for me. Nothing else. I am looking at the office wall. All the clips from Cherish. *What an amazing project*, I think.

But really. What is happening to my energy? I am at a lower frequency. But perhaps that is good. Relaxing. Deep relaxing. Feeling what moves in the body. Feeling how tired it is. After all, Cherish was only five months ago and then school and then Mexico. Perhaps this is just okay the way it is. Everything is as it should be. Be patient. Trust your nature. Accept yourself. That is the biggest change.

As mentioned earlier, Buckminster Fuller taught us that we are all astronauts aboard this spaceship earth. We are all part of the same ecosphere. We are all in this together, so we might just start caring for the Earth Mother that carries us all through space. But the moment is also a vessel. We are traveling together inside the eternal moment on the vast ocean called time. It might seem that we have left behind the old shore, and that new ones are waiting behind the horizon. That is how it looks to the one travelling through history, through the eternal moment. But in reality, the vast ocean of time exists in all its facets and all its dimensions regardless of our momentary positions on it. Time has depths that have not yet been fathomed. One drop of the ocean holds the same qualities as all of it. Like our eternal souls hold the same quality of the divine.

This morning I am thinking that it is okay to be tired. I managed to run the BA-program alone for the first year. I have made a list of all the things I need to do before summer. It's a nice list. Then I am thinking that this clearing out is really working. The drop of insight above simply dripped into my mind the other day. Sitting outside the sushi parlor with my daughter, I saw this holographic reality. I saw how we are not only on this Earth Mother together but bound to each other inside this eternal moment, rolling through time, traversing the huge landscape of time, that is coexisting, already there, existing.

That's a new bundle.

THE ROAD HOME

The way of the traveler
can only be written in water.

Each wave in the ocean
Has its own crevice.

Each soul its own path.

Like the stones on the beach.
Like the carpet of needles in the fir grove.

Like the rings made by rain in water.

Each cloud on the sky goes its own way.
It never comes back.
Each stream sings with its own voice.
It never repeats itself.

Each soul has its own path
Waiting to be taken up.

Beauty lives between things
As the virgin tending her garden.
Beauty is written on the sky
But is seen from below.

The little child playing in a puddle of water at dusk,
Oblivious to time, to all ends.

Rain connects heaven and earth
As streams of tears,
Columns of smoke.
Darkness covers you as a blanket.

GREAT-GRANDMOTHER AND ME

In the beginning—well, that is to say way before the beginning, on the way in, by the popcorn stall, during the commercials and the credits, before the movie even began—

Great-grandmother was, and at the same time she was not (except time had not been created yet back then),
so A didn't equal A; that is to say: A ≠ A.

Differences were shared to create, like when different genders share and from that comes new life, new identities;
Like the golden spiral, the Fibonacci count, the pentagram.
We see this in nature. The golden measure is in the petals of the sunflower, the spiral of the seashell, the cones of the pine tree.

In the leg of a frog.

Then the movie started.
(Wind Eagle says this was because Great-Grandmother became bored and bent back on herself and created Great-Grandfather.)

And suddenly, A did equal A. Hell yeah! We were straight inside the beginning and thought there had never been anything else.

In the beginning was the Word, and the Word was with God and God said let there be more light,
as if he had invented that himself.

Well, perhaps he did, but he sure didn't invent himself.

Suddenly, identity was used to speak of differences.

A = A.

And that was all there was to it. My shoes are shoes so that I can tell the difference between left and right.

Then we went straight on to identify the differences between black and white, man and woman, rich and poor, good and bad, right and wrong.

Instead of proportion and balance, instead of golden measure, we produced the grid and the coordinate system: I think, therefore I am. The system of identity, the cube where each side is exactly the same, the point without extension. Discrete units of like quantity so that we could "Lean" model the whole of the universe, making everything external to our own inner lives.

So we forgot about the great-grandmother, and we forgot that the left and the right cannot be reduced because the right and the left side of my brain aren't identical, and the great polarization began.

We all became interchangeable points on the grid, numbers in the flowchart, expendable, and no longer unique. A quantum.

And this is where they start rewinding the reel after the show is over

Because right down there in the smallest quantum, quality is all that matters.

So just remember, folks, if this cooks your noodle, that Grandma did the seats, the movie, wrote the script, did the wonder of projection, the timeframe, the building, and the street outside where you emerge after the show is over at dusk, where you still hear the voices of children playing in the long twilight of a summer's eve just like this.

TAO

The Tao te Ching states that
Before the general was the king.
Before the king was God,
And before God was Tao.

And she was perfect.

Speculating on intensive science,
One take is to see the Big Bang as a minor event.
Perhaps we can measure the depths of the black holes
Now that infinity has been restored to both ends of the stick.

If we see the big bang as a minor event.

A bump.
An energy bump on the road.

Tao means that,
The road.
So in the beginning was the Word, we say,
With the almighty Father.
And he said,
"Let there be light."

But it was just a bump, a light One
On the road.

Tao is the great-grandmother outside this time and space.
Of course, we can't know that
Because we can't see further than to the beginning.
That's when light for seeing was created.
Remember?

But Tao knows us,
Knows the road in darkness,
The road will take us.

And we will take to the road.

SOUTHBOUND

We have arrived at Easter, and I can feel the change in the energy. This morning I started with my morning pages, my tea and my yoga. The energy coming from the light is very strong now. Forgiveness, clarity, love. I feel the energy of Christ growing around us as the streets grow empty and the town is quiet on this Saturday afternoon. The color is yellow, and the light of love the same. A bright yellow shining in the daffodils, in the sun, in the yellow flame of the candle. I feel the forgiveness, I feel the grace, I feel the love of God almost bathing me as the sunshine does on the crisp spring day.

Opening the South practice was just like opening a gift that you have been waiting for. Perhaps it was too early, but I couldn't wait. My intuition told me that the Easter days would be a good time to receive this gift, to receive the gift of forgiving myself. And the teaching was not very far off either. Veronica and I had agreed to a complete stop of using media in our household. Morgan was departing for a friend's house during the holiday and asked if he could take his phone. I said no; my wife said yes. Then we had a situation. A scene. Even my eldest started saying that it didn't matter; my youngest said that we shouldn't quarrel.

In the end, the phone stayed home. Perhaps I should've softened up. At least taken responsibility for my emotions. I am listening to WindEagle as I think these thoughts. To embrace difference. Ready my stance. Realize the pattern of feeling alone and acting from it in affect. I guess I am right, but it's not about being right. It is about being whole.

Listening to all the voices. Respecting the differences. I could have been quiet. I could have been open. But I wasn't. I was strung out. In my own drama. I am letting the vibration of Easter into that. Transcending. On the rise. Asking what is needed for me to own my ground so that I can command my state.

SWAHA

I am studying the allies, which is part of the council guide training. I am seeing the polarity between the healer and the victim. Between superior mind and mystery, between shapeshifter and judge. The dissonance that I experienced through the Easter days has grown into ever so many standard arguments in my household. But I am distancing myself from them and resting in the quiet. I listen to the South wheel a lot, gradually understanding what it is about. Growing out of problems instead of trying to solve them. Accepting and appreciating circumstances instead of trying to change what has already manifested.

I am trying to be in the in-between. Entering the mystery through silence. Appreciating what is and ready for what wants to emerge. I am doing my morning practice. I am especially focusing on the fire blessing to keep my strength through the day. And I am standing, standing for the light, remembering that the first one I need to send light and love is myself. There is quite a continuity in this from East over Southeast, to South. In order to stay open. Stay open to see what gift comes in the guise of difference. What is there that I need to learn? In this difference, in this bias, in this prejudice, in this judgment? In the stupid commentary? In the degrading glance? In the indifferent smile? In the harsh voice? In the mean words?

Victim or healer? I am writing down the list of allies in my medicine book. Superior mind/great mystery, victim/healer, appreciator/devourer; I have all those. Both as allies and distorted faces, shadows, dark capes. So I embrace those, but I want to do that consciously. To be consciously in the victim and not go there by default. I want to use these three next weeks to go consciously into my victim, who is saying, "You are alone. You are not worth caring for. You are nothing." I want to embrace that and say, "I am at the center. I care for myself. I am one of the first. I have the best job in the world. At the center of the world, I know myself. I love myself. I am with God. Great Spirit, Jesus, Krishna, Holy Mary and Magdalene, Mother Earth, Great-Grandmother. That's whom I am working for. And I have the most beautiful woman. I cherish her. As she is. And I have great teachers in my wonderful kids, who both came here to teach and who need guidance. And our house is a gift. A gift from Krishna to bring us out of disharmony and into our own. We are in our own. I am not alone. I am at the center."

DOES HE HAVE MY TICKET?

Morgan has been away for three days. So I haven't been yelling for three days. Do not like to blame him, but more like a welcome break in order to step into my I am with him. Realizing that he is also South practice. Forcing me to be in my center instead of my anger. I'm thinking that he always has a long dialogue inside, and that part of this is what is annoying me because I sense the low frequency in these thoughts. They make me angry because I do not like to recognize them in myself. Perhaps I am the one who has the inner dialogue. So how can I talk to him about these feelings without outlawing them but with the opportunity for him to transcend into a higher state without having to fulfill the physical need that always accompanies his feeling? It's like I am feeling this. If I got that, I would get rid of that feeling, so I will ask for this or that thing. Allowing for the feelings of jealousy, anger, resentment, fear, sadness, loneliness. This is my mirror.

I think I am finally getting it. How dedicated you need to be in order to break a habit or pattern. I am looking into my relationship with my eldest again, knowing that all there ever was to learn about staying centered, staying aligned, staying open, embracing differences, embracing the distorted images of the allies, the shadow, the small I, the prisoner is right there. So come on. I am ready for you. Under no circumstances will I move from my center. Under no circumstances will I raise my voice. Under no circumstances will I end up as a victim of my emotions. I ready myself to see each potential conflict with my eldest as a teaching, a meditation. Is it hard? Does he have my ticket? Can he ring my bell? Well, Hell yeah. It is. He has. He does. But I am ready. I am open.

BLAME

I simply wanna get rid of blaming others, finding out whose fault it is. I wanna to get rid of trying to get to the bottom of the list. To get over with it. That's the old pattern. Let's get this life over with. This ordeal. Or this working day. Or this project. Or this assignment. The old pattern is thinking how to execute in order to get over with whatever, and the blaming whosoever gets in the way or doesn't conform to the timetable in my head. In order to go home and drown it all in the bottom of the bottle. The historical conscious man is always negative, says Walter Benjamin, because he knows that everything can at all times go wrong. Well, it's not like that. Everything is at it should be. I am trusting the process. I can't do anything wrong.

So what is this guilt? Where did it come from? This idea that there will be resolve when someone is found guilty. It's a primitive form of organization. It is the opposite of reaching for wholeness. I want to stop judging others. I can do that by keeping my words clean. I want to stop expecting from others. I can do that by stop presuming and stop taking things personally. Perhaps then I can see, see that everything is holy as it is. Perfect already. Illuminated from within.

And I start to learn. Staying open. Embracing difference. Learning and co-creating with the universe. This is a way of reaching for wholeness.

RADIANCE

What if the quality of the whole was more important than my own point of view? I am feeling that I have become radically better at getting out of arguments with my closest. I don't take things personally, so I don't end up in chain reactions. I pause. Take a deep breath. I remember it is a teaching. I ready myself. I open my self. I want to see the opposite view, the opposing argument. The other viewpoint. And the emotion. How does the other feel? I embrace that. I listen. I accept. Then comes a common understanding. Then comes a new foundation. A difference that we can share. I do this at home. With my son. With my woman. I do this at work. I listen. Profoundly. It is working. It is like a new trick, but it's not a trick. It is real.

It's like the world just became bigger. Don't take anything personally because everybody is living their own dreams or fantasies. Reaching for wholeness is like getting out of this fantasy. Waking up from this dream. The other person exists! The other person has his or her own take, emotions, and thoughts. Others are not just props or ready-made silhouettes or shadows in my personal fantasy or nightmare. They have they own realities, and I can bridge them. Expand into them. Be part of them by reaching for wholeness. So the world doubles. Becomes big again, as when I was a child. It becomes glowing, new, radiant. It becomes an adventure. A real fiction. The high dream.

HOPE

I have some lines that I do for my Southwest practice. I think this statement is what I stand on. What I stand for. The ground I am holding. The high ground. And it's a lot about hope. To hold the banner of hope in this well of darkness. Because that is how it looks when you lose hope. I was seeing selected scenes from *The Lord of the Rings* with my youngest son the other day, and the message of the book finally hit me with full force. How to survive industrialization. How to survive in this Kali Juga, the industrial age, the age of blood, greed, and death. In the film, Gandalf said, "There never was much hope, only a fool's hope." I am that fool, I am bringing that hope, I am holding that dream that we will have peace. Peace and one nation. All of us united. Everyone goes. When my grandchildren's children grow up to be men and women.

I am listening a lot to the energies. That they are not divided into good or bad feelings. Simply higher or lower vibrations as tones or qualities. This week I have been going down through all the old ones, all the lower ones, like nine circles of hell. My own private, self-created hell. I am trying to accept these lower feelings. Some of them are surely not my own, but I did let them become part of my life, and that past is still part of me, and I am embracing that. This is deep work, this hurt. To relive and reenact the most shameful things in my life in order to forgive it and let it go.

Shaking hell. I don't want to be a victim, but I want to embrace the victim that I was in order to stay in touch with both the black and the white wolf.

THE LOTTERY

So what's good about the black wolf allies? The devourer makes me go into things, like devouring a book or thought. What is good about the victim? For the healer to know what the person who is asking for help feels and what the person's outlook in life is. To be weak when weakness is most needed, to give away instead of breaking. For the judge to discern. For the superior mind to remember to be humble. For the drama queen to be flamboyant, to kick up dirt when that's all there is left. Do battle without raising the army. For the workhorse to dream and get things done. So how can I keep my peace with them when what I want to do is feed the white wolf? I can respect. Respect instead of condemn. Remember that it is simply lower energy, not bad, but a darker timbre, and sometimes those also come in handy in this life world.

I have been doing a lot of state altering. Simply trying to enter a room and change my state. Of course, in the family, going from angry irritated parent to an understanding, embracing one. And yes, it works. At work I have realized that I am an administrator. I am holding the high dream, bringing hope while administrating. So I am trying to take all the victim energy out of the budget cuts that I can surf all right but that also needs to be administrated. And that can be a lot. So I am changing state by claiming this as my lot. This is the lottery ticket. This is the lot I chose. I won this.

And like Lao Tse, who is the great-grandfather of administration, or Kafka, who worked every day in an insurance company, writing at night, I cherish this post. I hold it.

FALL

Today I was at the harvest moon ceremony with Singing Woolf and EagleHeart. My eldest son and I went, and we took a medicine walk, in part to find a medicine name for him, in part to reconcile our father and son conflict and to celebrate abundance.

We went up a little stream near an old quarry for whitewash in Farum, very beautiful, called Hestehave, meaning the garden of horses.

Walking midstream in our Wellingtons, we encountered this beautiful bird, a heron. The bird led us on. Then it disappeared, then it showed us a bridge, then it disappeared. Walking along the small river, we finally encountered it on the opposite shore. Singing Woolf had told us of two people, opponents standing on two facing shores, and our obligation to stand forth, to go into that river.

So we did. We got soaked, water pouring into our rubber boots, but we followed suit and found a garden of paradise, a swamp or bog but with small bridges and pagodas for the heron, and a small island with a couple of beach chairs and a strange hanging thing. A table, we realized, that could be lowered and used as a coffee table.

Sitting there, rejoicing on the journey and the good medicine of the heron, we thought, *Wouldn't it be good with a soda or a snack?* We hadn't brought anything, but there was a strange box-like instalment. I asked my son to investigate, and ho! An abundance of sofa, waffles, crackers, even beer materialized!

Along with a small ledger inviting us to share as long as we also share our experiences. ♥ We did, and we saw this as deep teachings on the nature of the universe, of time, of gifting, and of the sacred sweet medicine.

SORROW

Today I felt like doing all the things that aren't good for me: drinking, smoking, eating meat, sugar, coffee, being weak, melancholic and staying home, slobbering. I recognize this frailty as the other side of my light being, this deep well of sorrow in me.

I drew a card from my new deck, the Guardians of Light. I drew the justice card, not as in placing guilt—believe me, this deep drive in me creates it all right—but in respect for all included in this relation of sorrow.

In my meditation I asked, "Where does this sorrow come from? To whom does it belong?" I realized that the sorrow comes from my parents, for not having been able to make a successful marriage and to step out of the shadow of their parents, who did stay together, albeit for worse better than for good. The sorrow came to me as a child, almost as a force of nature, as a deep disappointment and melancholia because I really loved my parents and wished the best for them. The sorrow is in my brothers, whom I also love but who, like me, live lonely and uncompassionate lives.

I realized all this, and I prayed for forgiveness for all of us: Grandmother and Granddad on both sides, my father and mother, my brothers and me, and for the effect on my spouse and children. I prayed for forgiveness and for lifting this spell on all of us, physically, spiritually, mentally, and emotionally in all our pasts, presents, and futures.

I prayed for the Great Spirit to let me realize the difference between the experience of deep sorrow and my true nature. I prayed for letting me see this gift in its true light. To let me harvest its wisdom. To replace my experience of family life and as rational, alienated, devoid of inner life and filled with sorrow, regret, and impotence with the opposite. To be able to create a space for my own family and society filled with warmth, love, meaning, purpose, respect, and acknowledgment.

I hold this to be the truth. That I am not any longer identical with this experience, that I never was, but that I have learned from this and that I am able to create a relationship within my family that is filled with light, harmony, wisdom, teaching, and divine peace.

MOTHER

I am grateful for you.
I am grateful for the life you gave me.

Growing up in the forest,
Learning the love of the ocean.

I am grateful for the bad times.

It has made me choose
If I want to live or die.

To wake up and incarnate.

It must have been a lonely task,
Teaching me this.

But I am grateful for the teaching.
No other teacher would have succeeded in this.

So please don't blame yourself
About the past.

I know what you went through because I went there myself.
So drunk my kids don't recognize me anymore,
Like Noah in the vineyard.

I embrace that.

There is nothing good or bad.
Everything is as it should be.
Everything is light.

I love you

FATHER

The sun is riding in the sky field,
And dawn has come.

We have been waiting
All night.

I am reading aloud to you.

The tale of how the robin got its color.

How it hid in the bushes,
Ashamed
To be gray.

How it waited
Till one day
It saw
Christ.

With his crown of thorns.

And as
It pulled a thorn from his brow,
Blood
Spilled on the breast of the small bird.

That's how it got its color, you know.

I was crying as I read this aloud to you,
and I am crying
as I write these lines for you.

BACK IN BLACK

The house is very quiet these days since My wife and eldest have left. Actually, they have very restless energy. On the other hand, I let the kids watch their shows on the telly. As I did before. I would cook, drink, do stuff in the house and tussle around, and then drink some more. Now it's hard for me to estimate how much Veronica was actually there. Of course, she was there while the kids where babies, but after that? My recollection is that she spent lots of time at her workshop and with the different classes she took, being away several weekends. Not that it matters. Now we are trying to be a real family, and it is a hard awakening. We did a family vision; we have a family council. Veronica and I started sleeping together again. So we are changing, but we laid the foundation for something else. That means that we also need to change that foundation. The early years are still in the kids, with me drinking and my wife being absent. Two absentminded parants. I think my eldest son is taking the hardest toll on this one, using the emergent space to call for attention. But who knows? And what about me? So I threw away the bottle, great achievement, and good for the kids to experience. But sometimes I feel that I am continuing some of the patterns that I learned from my mother when she was raising us alone. Well, why shouldn't I? Because you are not alone anymore. I am not alone. I don't need to rely on the single mom bribe and pamper strategy. So what does a dad do?

On another level, I am finding out that there is a whole new palette of things that I need to consider. The difference between yoga or not. The difference between coming or not while having sex. The difference between morning practice or not. But also what I am eating. Sweets are just like alcohol; well, in fact, they are alcohol. The impact of media, watching pornography for instance. All these things are filling my energy field with a low vibration. Is this what I want? Why am I choosing this? Because I feel sorry for myself? Because I feel I have deserved it? This is not me. This is not who I am choosing to be. And then it is. Perhaps I am no longer the victim; I was the victim, but it is a part of my story. The problem seems to be when the victim and the devourer team up; then things go down. Well, what are their positive parts? The victim is the healer, so when I have used up my healing energy without regenerating, I go over.

And the devourer? It's the appreciator. The one who accepts the situation without feeling sorry for himself or herself and also the one who can appreciate a single sweet or one cup of coffee. So it is about balancing the allies and respecting them, while also recognizing their shadow sides and making room for them.

Okay. So we have allies and distorted capes. Or well, the same ally depending on if you feed the black or the white wolf. I guess both need to be fed if you want to avoid ending up in the ditch with one of them. But like the ego holds my knowledge of this life and my ability to communicate with the others in this dream, the black wolf and the distorted capes must also hold their values. No one has yet told us what Boggie Street is for? After all, what is a good man but a bad man's teacher? We are all going this time; no one stays behind. This is the only place they serve coffee in this universe. I love the story about the disciple who said that I am really not worried about my own salvation or my coming lives; I only want to serve in whatever position the Lord chooses for me. What I am worried about are all those fools out there, not even knowing that they are condemned already. For those people I worry. So please let everyone of them wake up, and let me stay here on this plane until the last one of them has met your grace. I am one of those fools. Even Dalai Lama had to eat meat once, when he was sick, in order to regain his strength. So we need the shadow. We must become conscious of what rests therein so that we are not unconsciously exercising it on others but using it to show our own vulnerabilities to others. That is actually the greatest teaching I have from WindEagle, to remain in my humanity, in the weakness of my flesh.

Waking up this morning, I find I am still alive on this planet. So there is a cloud of happiness around me along with the tiredness. I am really letting myself go into that. Seeing how deep it is. Just relaxing with Vega and Elias. I am absentminded, slack, letting go. It's almost like a detox, just the other way around. It has lasted since mid-February, with the Mexico trip as an intermezzo. I haven't realized how much this last year has taken of me. It feels like I have lost all my initiative, or I just have to follow this sinking feeling to see what is there. To follow the chi right down to the center of Mother Earth, waiting for her to send back the energy. I had thought, really, that the end of kiva time would also mark a return of energy and vitality, but it has been the other way around. I have been resting in this slackness. Accepting that my body and small I need to be heard, need the rest, the slowness, and the low-energy frequency. But this morning there was a certain glow around me. Remembering waking up early, feeling that the world was good, this life was good, feeling that I could do anything. In my mind, I need to wake up at four thirty to do morning pages and yoga. But that is just in my mind. Right now, I need to rest with what is. To grasp the remains of these self-destructive and negative thoughts and patterns hidden in the small cups of my mind's bowels.

Wauw, now I see it. This is the "normal" state of mind. This is what I started drinking to get away from. This is why I was smoking forty a day and drinking ten cups of coffee just to get down again with a bottle of red wine, as long as that was enough. Well stable, sort of, on this self-medication. Drunk on self-perception and punished by desire. It's the dreary, gray, iron grasp of so-called everyday reality routine. It's everything I let other people plant in my garden of consciousness running wild as weeds on a vacant lot left to itself. It's everything I was told I can't do because I am not smart enough, brave enough, strong enough, good enough. Because I am not enough. It's the utter boredom of being trapped inside a second-rate version of yourself created by the thoughtless comments of others, by well-meaning teachers, capitalist media, and parents without any clues about parenting. It's utterly numbing. It's like the outside weight of societal demands asking you to conform, do your duty, perform, compete, without any overlaying ideology or spiritual matrix. Perhaps there were one once, in church, in the nation, but now it seems there is only the role of consuming. Being numbed out by self-judgment, by lack of natural stimulus. Instead, it is filled with poison from food, air, media. But I am enough. Radically self-appreciatingly enough. Just like I am.

And it is a story about energy practices, what brings down the vibration and the level of energy, and what heightens the vibration and creates surplus. It's about how energy can be drained, and it's about how energy can be restored. And it is about how energy can be stable. How energy comes from emotion, and how my emotions can become stable. Yoga, morning practice, morning pages, going to meditate, holding a strict diet, fire blessing, filling up with light during the day, tantra: All these are methods to heighten my vibration, like hot air and ballast in an air balloon. While coffee, sweets, alcohol, meat, media, and ejaculation are means to lower my vibrations.

So it is the little child who grew up into a straitjacket of misconceived ideas and concepts void of real meaning. And the why stopped after a while to be replaced by the what. Senseless in a senseless world, corrupted in every sense of the word. Then the joy of life—the spontaneous joy of being, running, playing—disappears, and with that, only duty and conformity are left. Long dreary days of reading senseless e-mails and doing pseudo-work in the control state. So how can I reawaken my little child? Not the inner child; that's something else, the cousin of victim. No, the inner child, who can now depend on the warrior to play in safety and laugh in the face of blizzards and buzzards. How can I awaken him? Come on, little child, wake up to play. Wake up and see it is a new morning. Wake up with these morning pages. I'll teach you how to write, and we can write a story together.

What would that story be like? Lying with Elias yesterday and talking about Granddad's death, I suddenly felt him as presence. Very lovingly, filled with golden warm energy and with a soft dignity. I know that this is one of the realities about us. Our souls manifested in this lifetime. A sort of avatar, but very easy to identify with and relate to. How can I become this glowing loving energy that I already am in this lifetime?

Listening to my youngest son's memories about Granddad and his feelings about death, I was suddenly reminded of my own little child and tried to console his in his grief. The sensitivity. The sincerity. The simplicity. Being completely present in his emotions. Being true to his emotions. Not trying to run away or hide. But simply facing it. Resting in it. Being true to yourself.

I have the impression that this here earth is a school for angels. That we are all in training. And just like the school I am working on myself, people graduate and find their way. I also have the sense that all materials are living materials, and they all have a soul to carry. We are simply here to co-create with Mother Nature, creating a beautiful nature in ourselves and taking care of her beauty as her servants.

I am thinking that the coming years will bring much turmoil. But I am also feeling the rebellious spirit of taking a stand against everything that is moving in the wrong direction. Radical self-acceptance. I am not worried about this at all. Being here in Denmark feels safe. The idea that the forest where I grew up is a special place, where energy beings are building a center of knowledge and understanding, has a deep resonance with me. Yesterday I was at a lecture about this, and I was deeply touched. Another thing that touched me was that my mother, who just lost her husband, told me that between Easter and Pentecost, Jesus is actually walking on this earth. I find that idea deep and beautiful.

Yesterday I was reminded how much my work has an influence on me. I was talking to my eldest son's teacher and seeing the same pattern. My son uses all his energy at school and then comes home. I do the same under the pretense that I can relax when I come home. That is the old abuser thinking. Instead, I need to shift, allowing time and energy for all the tasks at home in order to keep my base safe and stable, cozy and clean. I am also seeing very clearly that all the arguments between the kids comes from Veronica's and my disagreements. We need to bury these weapons, not just talk about it. Then happiness will come back to stay.

I was also taking a long walk in the woods alone. I was lying on the ancient sacrificial stone from the bronze age, letting go of the last of my victimhood. I know it is part of the black wolf–white wolf allies of healer and victim, but I need to be able to step into them consciously and not as a default. I was doing that at work, and that is why it got to me. I was feeding the black wolf. I am alone, I am taking the last stand, I am a victim of the budget-cuts, I am a victim of my boss's attempt to micromanage everything, and so on. But it is not like that. I chose those cuts as a teacher, teaching me to become conscious of how I identify with work. If only there was enough money I would. That is not the truth. The truth is I need to learn that I am not that job. I am not a victim. I am free and strong.

Quitting smoking was the best and hardest decision in my life. It was a decision every day for three and a half years, and then it was a living hell with drinking for another three and a half years. But now I can actually do what I always wanted. Smoke a single cigarette and then forget about it. I didn't drink for one and a half years, and then yesterday I had a beer, simply because I felt like it.

Okay, does that mean I am back in line? In Mexico, I had the same sensation—that I was free, that I could do what I like. So I didn't do anything. Well now I did. It was strange. On one hand, I felt that the drops in energy the last weeks and months were partly due to the fact that I postponed doing this, overcoming my fear. And there is fear. Fear of polluting my new clarity, fear of going back down the hole. I even dream of it, that I took a drink by accident. Just like yesterday. I am at a party, drinking, and then suddenly, I wake up and find out that it is a dream. Well, a nightmare, that is. Now I am not gonna wake up. This is real. So how do I feel about it? How was it? Well, it was okay. I don't think I'll run straight to the kiosk for more. Afterward, it was a sort of slippery, nasty feeling. So that's pretty certain. But what about the next arrangement or party?

Well, I still don't know. Not drinking at these things was always a bit awkward, but hey, I managed. What really struck me was how much drinking alcohol resembles eating sugar. Wow, so much of the addiction is bound up in the sugar. So being a sugar junky is not healthy either. I know that, but now it has a much deeper meaning. How can I drop all these stimulants and stay clean? It has a lot to do with the allies, especially the devourer. Staying in the middle, on the golden road, as with the monthly smoke. But it seems hard for me when it comes to sugar, let alone alcohol or coffee. So it is better for me to just stay off limits. But going full force into yoga, herbal tea, and veggies can also be an aspect of the devourer but in a healing dimension. I wish I could take the energy off these matters and quit with sugar and alcohol, just as I did with the smokes.

I wake up in the middle of the night with the acute sense that this was an one and only tryout. I guess it was like that with the smokes. The fear of ending up in the drain once again. But I didn't; I don't. I remember Venice, not drinking though I was with My old boss who were constantly drinking and asking me why I didn't. Complaining that I didn't. Then I remember Maputo, where I didn't drink even though there were great times with the locals. In Japan. In Mexico, where I felt I could do it. So it is no problem. Then why does it feel like a problem? It's staying in the middle, I guess, and below that, the maturity to choose my state. I'm not drinking because it lowers my energy. I'm not eating sugar and meat because they lower my energy. I'm not drinking coffee because it drains my system, and that lowers my energy. Low energy isn't bad. It's just low. I'm doing yoga, drinking tea, and eating vegetables because they give me a high energy level. That's not good. It's just high. So staying there all the time also means that you lose your grounding if you are not able to use your allies in both the white and the black shapes. How can I respect my fragility without giving way to bad habits? How can I stay on the middle of the road? Or consciously choose to stay in the upper register while not condemning the lower? In a sense, it was the same with the two months I did tantra every day. I did not wish to let go of my physical pleasure, satisfying myself while practicing continence.

Yesterday I was revisiting the zone. While I was there, I drew a chart of what has happened the last two years. So many things have happened, from the portal gathering in Lalita, where I made my quest. Be patient. Trust your nature. Change yourself. And I have. To a great extent, changed. We have moved. We have made the Cherish project. I have become my own boss. We have traveled in Japan, India, and Mexico. I have done the first year of evocative leadership and a series of modules to become a medicine man. We have gone to Sundance. Veronica and I have started to change our relationship. We have taken up tantra. She has gotten a PhD grant, and the order book is full.

The last months I have felt very tired, and now I understand why. We achieved many things. Just sitting here, I also feel that there were things left behind that I needed to revisit in order to embrace them. In order to let go of the guilt. In order to accept that these traits are part of me. Whether they belong to me or not, I chose to let them rule my life. I chose to let them protect me until I was ready. Yesterday they were telling me to be more honest, to be fully honest with this writing for instance.

So it ends like it began. This morning we got ready to cast a new concrete floor in our basement. One and a half years ago, we started that while I was lying in a stupor of liquor, trying to recover from the failed Venice trip. Like a double dip. Only worse. Or déjà vu. Or a flash back. The last week has been a revisiting the old places of my own personal hell. Of not knowing the boundary of self-indulgence, self-pity, gluttony, escapism. I really got back down. To feeling the pain that comes from having to vomit as you get up. Of how it hurt your stomach when you start the morning at six o'clock with a pilsner. I got down through all the mud, the guilt, the shame, the having to count what you drank in order to ride the card. All those dirty little economics and reckonings that come with drinking. And so here I am, out of it again. It was a short visit.

So what is good about it, except that it was short? I feel I am humbler now. I see how far I have come. I see how hard it is. I understand the pain. And I see that the limitless nature of my abuse can be found in other venues of my life. I don't have to tackle it or come to grips with it in the arena of alcohol. I can choose one of the others because basically, this is about feeling alone, feeling that I am not worth caring for, that I would rather be dead. And in some of the things I do when I am walking straight, I am still killing my own flame. Why am I doing this? To prove that I am not worthy? Or to feel sorry for myself? I want to protect my sacred flame from now on. So I pray for forgiveness. Now I have looked in the dark mirror, and I accept what I see by writing these lines. I embrace it. Then I would like to pray to Jesus for letting this pattern be replaced with another; I care for myself. I am protecting my own sacred fire.

This morning I felt that something has changed. That the transformation that was promised in the kiva has begun. From the deepest cavern of my soul to the pinnacle of my spirit, dawn has come.

Taking the Metro to the rainbow ceremony and then across Europe to Frankfurt. Yesterday I did a long cleansing ceremony in the sauna and in the ocean. I had many answers. Last week was simply a final look in the dark mirror separating the old me and the new. Not that there's anything bad or judgmental about it. It was simply just two different states. I had a deep look into the gluttony and devourer, which is basically about escaping this plane because it hurts, and I can't stand the pain. I know it is a birth trauma, but when I am clean and in my high-energy self, I can easily stand the pain. I saw my bird, the Camorant, and he showed me once again to dig deep, to dive deeper into myself, my soul, and beyond. As long as I am with this energy, I will always find my way, and I won't feed the black wolf in this, which is the gluttony aspect. The pathfinder loses his way and wants to escape the path he chose for himself. An angle shy of hell.

In the West, I asked what is needed to make the shift I want, to stop judging and start respecting, to stop expecting and start taking responsibility, to see that everything is holy and that everything that meets me is a teaching and a gift of learning. In order to make this shift, I need to give to myself first. So simple. That was what I was doing yesterday while in the South, also getting close with my drama queen. I'm always left on my own. I am the only one helping here; I give to you, but you never give back. I am trying to marry her off to my inner adventurer.

Concluding my meditation, I felt very vividly that Aurora was in direct alignment with me and ready to come down. That night we prayed for blessings and to be of service, and we made love. Now it is up to Spirit and the holy Virgin to decide.

Out of the rainbowlodge with fire in my hair and a shining, glowing heart. In there I let out all my anger and frustration. Now I am listening to WindEagles's South podcast again, trying to apply it to my work situation. They had me on my knees, but now I am back. How can I protect myself and my energy? How can I embrace the difference of incompetence? How can I lean into administrating? How can I learn to love the list? I know why I am here. In the lodge, one of my students came to thank me for holding the space for them. She came in her spirit form. As her true self. An emissary.

The lion of Zion came to me with softness and love and his flaming mane. To both his sides the white buffalo woman and the lamb were walking with him. Below, the Earth Mother held him, and above, the Great-Grandmother. To each of the directions, Krishna, Great Spirit, Virgin Mary, and Mary Magdalena were holding him. His force is in me to support and hold me and never let me fail.

This morning I have a deep teaching in stepping in between. Yesterday we were doing the sharing on the South intelligence, and I heard many aspects of this that were not yet in my focus. To remember to step into the in-between, that I don't have to react to anything, anything at all. This morning, Veronica was first apologetic that she was too tired to be intimate, and then she rejected me. At once I was in my reaction, but then I saw I don't have to react to that or even respond. I can just let it go, realizing that she is in affect and letting her find out how she will deal with that. It's simple, really. Just don't connect. Don't get tricked into it. Just let go. Realize that she is emerged in her emotional reality, in her own drama. It has nothing to do with me.

Another point in the emotional intelligence has to do with difference. As I embrace this experience and the unpleasant emotion of feeling rejected, I also sense my own worth anew. It shows me the wholeness of my emotion, to stay stable, to rest in my own appreciation of myself. Wholeness is only experienced through diversity. Wholeness, meaning holy, meaning whole. To see the gift of difference. To experience wholeness. To be able to reach for wholeness. That is what I want, reach for wholeness through appreciating difference. And then to remember that every time I feel hurt, there is a space for healing, and beyond that healing, there is a value, something that I stand on. There is the high ground. So weeding my garden of consciousness, healing the soil, and understanding what wants to emerge as a true value is the high ground.

I have been out of the loop. Well, that is writing a lot in my deepening journey, but neglecting to do morning pages. In the weekend, I was doing the final workshop with Magic Moonwolf, concentrating on power animals, knowledge, and instinct. I really felt good, but I must admit that family and work had me crawling on all four after two days. Two days! That's what it takes for my family and work to peel all the medicine out of me and have me reacting and being victim to my emotions. I made a big scene here and at work, though in both cases, new ideas and change came out of it. My wife realized that we need a new kind of organization. At work, my boss gave up the grownup auditorium. So I can trust my emotions to make the changes I need.

During ceremony yesterday, I went deep into these matters. I do not want to end up in my victim energy. I even found a new space in my body, teaching me when I am in that. My left shoulder. I was working with not letting my work interfere with my personal life, envisioning the days I need to be there as separate from my other life. I need to make a clear division. I felt clearly that I am not a victim. I do not want to behave or be treated like one. On the other hand, I am grateful that Veronica holds her PhD, that the school made Cherish possible, and that it is facilitating my medicine work. So it is about making a balance between private and personal lives and my working life. The school is not me. It is not my identity. I do not wish to identify with it any longer. My true identity is different. It has nothing to do with the academy. I wrote this in the "true story," and today I want to translate that into English.

I have been doing all this writing to clear out my channel, but somehow, it seems that it has become more cluttered in the process. As the study year comes to a hold, I find myself worn-out completely. I am reading the above, realizing the truth in this, but also feeling even more a victim of this circumstance than ever before. I feel a prisoner in this job, in this family, in this city. I feel bound, I feel trapped, but I want to feel free, to break free.

Yesterday I had a big quarrel with my wife again. For her letting me do all the chores in the morning, I have been simply going on, not feeling my own boundary has been crosses. And then, in the weekend, I stayed with my daughter in the countryside, trying to rejuvenate. But coming back to the city, all this meditation was simply washed away with the low-energy frequency of this family.

In the car going to an old friend's, I did several meditations, trying to become the hollow bone. I tried to release all my pent-up anger, all my disgust. I tried to alter my state. State-changing.

In the end, we had a strange truce. My wife asked if I would like to go to the States for a whole year. I have thought that impossible, but in my present condition, I feel that a year off is just what I need. One more school year, and then I am off for a year of solitude, vacationing, resting, writing, and seeing inside. This morning it sounds like exactly what I need in order to come to myself again. Come into my own again.

I am alone. At last. The school is over, and I am alone in my small cabin. Today is ceremony day. I want to conclude my Southwest direction teaching about pathfinding intelligence. During the last month I have been taking time off to do these teachings, walking in nature, asking, "Who am I? What have I come here to be and become? What does my spirit long to manifest? What is my highest potential in this lifetime?" I have been drawing a big circle in the sand and walking the seven life circles that I am concluding now. Midway. I have been drawing all of them on a big piece of paper, and I have been seeing into the next seven circles and beyond. I have been learning that at school, I am also in school. Trying to learn how to create a harmonious atmosphere and society. I have seen that I will need this experience when I come back. I have been translating my new story into English to have it as a high-ground statement, a statement for the ground I am holding, for what I stand.

So now I am here. I actually managed the first year alone. I made many things. I spent all my energy, and now I am asking the Great Mother to receive the rest of my burdens and fill me with new energy to go another round around the sun. As I am sitting here, very much is about letting go and clearing emotions and thought patterns that prevent me from becoming the hollow bone.

Anger for instance, against my two sons. Where does that come from? I know it is helping me to ask my wife to step into family-life, so I am thankful for you, anger. But I am ashamed of the times I have been upset and yelled at my sons. I don't need this anymore. I am ready to forgive myself and let go of my anger, my shame. Just reading of Buddha, I notice that it is not about the difference in identifying with good or bad emotions. It is about identifying with emotions. They are transient, and I am not. I am eternal. I am limitless. I am the clear spring returning. So I want to release you, anger. And I release blame, guilt, shame, separation, hate, fear, neglect as well. I salute you. But in order to step into my own, I need to let you go. To become the hollow bone. To be whole. To be holy. To let love, benevolence, appreciation, joy, insight, compassion flow freely through me. From the Great Spirit to the Earth Mother, and from the Earth Mother and back to the cosmos and the Great-Grandmother. Steeping into my incarnation as a carrier of light has a lot to do with this. With responsibility. With taking responsibility for myself. My choices. The path I have chosen to walk. It has to do with enjoyment. Knowing my boundary. The yogini are eternally enjoying; they have complete knowledge and unconditional love because they are not trying to find these things here in the conditional and material world. Become transcendental to the three qualities of the material world: goodness, passion, and ignorance. Embrace true enjoyment, true love, and true knowledge. True in the sense that they are real, real in the sense that they are eternal.

Today I am making a ceremony of dedication of potential. Dedicating myself to remember. Remember who I am. Who we are. Becoming the hollow bone, the whole, the holy. To respond to the answers I have been calling in by questing. To claim them as mine. To be responsible. To walk my destiny. To be thankful. To listen to the voice of my spirit yearning. To see the continuity of my life unfold. To hold the high ground. To dedicate myself to walking this path. The path of beauty. The beauty way.

TWENTY COUNT

I am breathing in the energy of the sacred grandfather sun,
Welcoming in the power of light in my life.

I am breathing in the energy of the sacred Earth Mother,
Welcoming in the power of balance in my life.

I am breathing in the energy of the sacred plants,
Welcoming in the power of growth in my life.

I am breathing in the energy of the sacred animals,
Welcoming in the power of knowing in my life.

I am breathing in the energy of the sacred human,
Welcoming in the power of truth in my life.

I am breathing in the energy of the sacred ancestor spirits,
Welcoming in the power of presence in my life.

I am breathing in the energy of the sacred dream of life,
Welcoming in the power of remembrance and remembering who I am.

I am breathing in the energy of the cycles of law and the law of cycles,
Welcoming in interrelatedness.

I am breathing in the energy of the movement moon,
Welcoming in the power of change.

I am breathing in the energy of the higher Self,
Welcoming in the power of higher consciousness.

I am breathing in the energy of the sacred stars,
Welcoming in the power of the all potential.

I am breathing in the energy of the sacred planets,
Welcoming in their guiding power.

I am breathing in the energy of the sacred white buffalo woman,
Welcoming in the power of prayer.

I am breathing in the energy of the sacred sweet medicine,
Welcoming in the power of universal truth.

I am breathing in the energy of everyone who has lived, are living now,
will come to live,
Welcoming in the power of collective wisdom.

I am breathing in the energy of the great teachers,
Welcoming in the power of oneness.

I am breathing in the energy of the sacred kachinas,
Welcoming in the power of awakening.

I am breathing in the energy of the sacred avatars and great karma
masters,
Welcoming in the power of dreaming.

I am breathing in the energy of sacred pure science,
Welcoming in the power of evolving.

I am breathing in the energy of the Great Spirit,
Welcoming in the power of love.

STANDING MY GROUND

I am bringing forth my light.
I am illuminating the way.
I am holding the high dream.
I am walking the way of beauty.
I am seeing with love.
I am weighing the energies.
I am acting from my heart.
I bring hope.
I am free.
I am whole

TUNING IN

Sitting in my car, listening to the call for all the star captains to tune in. I am seeing it all, riding in my car, taking it all in. The minute details, the emergence and disappearance of the ten thousand things, usually overcast by habitual use and the wear and tear of the everyday humdrum. Today I am pretending I have landed in the previous century, in Paris perhaps, around 1900. I am noticing all the small things, all the details of street-life, all the rustics, all the people milling around, minding their own business. Just think if you were a time traveler, visiting this time and life. Now 2019. How you would cherish people standing at the bus stop in their streetwear, the dull advertisements, the cars queuing up—still using fossil fuel—the impatient businessman in the car next to you, the children on the bus, a young girl dreaming by the windowsill. A businesswoman in her suit and brand-new Audi A6, like a lioness, impatient. A young mother late for work with her kid on the back-saddle, risking her life for a moment in an ill-considered turn of the bike. Lorries. Bikes. Pedestrians. Everybody on their way. Mobilized as if there was a war going on. And the massage parlor with the Thai girls having the open sign already shining at eight o'clock in the morning. Just imagine being a time traveler. Well, you are. Traveler. Of time. And so am I. Even this worldly vessel on my spirit journey. The bride stripped naked for her bachelors. The table laid ready in the wilderness. In my car, riding and remembering Leonard Cohen's words:

> The stories of the street are mine, the Spanish voices laugh.
> The Cadillacs go creeping now through the night and the poison gas,
> O lady with your legs so fine O stranger at your wheel,
> You are locked into your suffering and your pleasures are the seal.
>
> With one hand on the hexagram and one hand on the girl I balance on a wishing well that all men call the world.

We are so small between the stars, so large against the sky, and lost among the subway crowds I try to catch your eye.
Leonard Cohen, *Stories of the Street*

IN THE METRO

In the metro with my two boys. My youngest son is off for camp but has forgotten his raincoat and his water bottle. I lose my temper. In the metro. In front of the crowd. We go back and hardly make the train with his class. In retrospect, I could have asked my eldest to donate his coat. Hell, the Flagcatchers for the coming PM election were even handing out free water bottles at Central Station, and in the end, the weather forecast turned against the 70 percent rain and thunder, and the sun stayed out to play all day, ending up at 29 degrees Celsius. Too hot for an argument. I can hear the Great-Grandmother laughing at me, trying in her own way to teach me. That it is already taken care of. That I just have to follow Tao. The way is unfolding; the tracks have been laid. I just have to cool off and remember. Remember the limitless nature of my soul. Trust my nature, not my temper.

So what teaching did I forget? Simple, to give to myself before I give to others. On my way to work, I realize this. My anger is projected onto a lot of external things, but the real crux lies in the fact that I have not made any space for myself recently. This morning was meant to be a lot of checking of the juhhuu list, but I reschedule. I turn the car around and head for the ocean, for solitude, for me-space. As I enter my meditation, it comes back to me in ever so many facets and from all eight directions: You have to give to yourself before you can give to others. I have been holding my wife for all the month of May since she was doing three exhibitions at the same time. But afterward, I focused on her being worn-out instead of looking to my own needs. When I fail to serve myself first, I even fail to take care of my kids. At the ocean I am reminded of these circles. My circle. My wife and mine. Our family. The work I have to do. In this order I hear Diamond light echo rainbow hawk; it may be a lot of work, but I don't see it that way. It's just me living my life.

HOLLOW BONE

The hollow bone is coming back to me. Not as a metaphor, but literally. I feel how it is when the marrow is filled with lower vibrations, and I sense the difference of consciously letting go and releasing all this pent-up emotion and giving it to the Earth Mother, who will in turn transform it to something new. As a conscious decision, I am not going to be negative, in my victim, in my anger, in affect, in denial. I am going to let go of these emotions, even though they make me feel secure, even though they are my habit, even though I identify with them. I release them. I let them go, and I feel the hollowness, the space they leave behind, and I try not to fill it. I try to stay hollow, to let the light run through me. To be profoundly open. To what is. To what wants to emerge. For situations to evolve. For the teaching to manifest. To sense the energy in the field. To receive and create from what comes to me by itself.

From this perspective, I can divide things into two distinct categories. The things I do to fill up the empty space, the hollow bone, and the things I do that give me energy to hold open the empty space instead of being afraid of it.

Satisfying material needs seem to belong to the first order. Sweets, media, coffee, meat, alcohol, smokes, and, I hate to admit it, ice-cream. The Hindu people say it straight out, the tongue is the hardest sense to discipline, not the ears, not the eyes, but the tongue. It is insaturable, both for slander and stimulus. In the second order, I find my writing. I find nature. I find solitude. I find this deepening journey. I find yoga. I find my medicine family. All of these help me to have the courage to stay open, to let the hollow space inside grow and grow. Wider, deeper, longer. To stay relaxed, to not tighten up, to have the energy to listen, and the instinct to act in the split-second when it is needed as an animal lying in wait.

THE OLD PATH

In a busy period just before the exams, I remember the sacred path of the botanical garden that I was taught years ago. To start from left to right, walking the circle, starting at the medical plant garden, walking up to the small mountain flora hill, meditating at the stream, going down to the crystal palace, crossing the bridge, taking the walk past all the statues in the patio. I am entering the garden. Remembering the sacred questing questions. Who am I? What am I here to be and become? What is my spirit yearning to express and manifest? What is my highest potential in this lifetime? I am simply holding them. Not trying to answer but only to hold. Answers come from nature, but I am not clinging to them. In this period, we have a long span before we start the West direction, and I decide to give myself the extra space. To go deep. To hold the questions. To do the practices. Questing for the sacred. Walking my destiny. Listening to the river of my sacred self. Drawing the red thread. Dedicating to potential.

I am meditating by the small stream, letting my troubles be washed away by the voice of the water. I am listening to the past, remembering who taught me to do this walk in the botanical garden. My old mentor. I hold this teaching sacred. I do the walk. At the bridge I make a detour, and I walk along the lake. Here I meet a heron standing by the shore of the lake. I watch as it repositions itself to avoid all the attention from the bypassers. I watch it as I repeat the questions that I am holding. And the heron answers me. It gives me its medicine: "Do not reject the past because in this you will only hold onto it even tighter. Accept the past as the path that led you here. The path you needed to take to come here and become the hollow bone. Then you can release it."

PYTHAGORAS

As I start my week, I go to the ocean to meditate, but the sauna is closed. I have been to the countryside to do a ceremony with the animal kingdom. Accessing knowledge, the power of knowing the four. And the fourteen. We have been drumming *in* power animals for all of our chakras. I am feeling centered again, and as my plans are washed away by the maintenance people of the sauna, I decide to drive further up the coast to do the spiral walk of destiny. At Bellevue, I get out and walk to the oceanside. It is raining mildly, and the beach is deserted. Some people relaying the tarmac are sleeping in their vehicles since you can't lay asphalt when it's raining. I take a long stick from my car and draw nineteen large circles in the sand. Each of them has seven-year periods, like I have been taught by Pythagoras. The first seven are almost concluded, and as I am walking those, I relive the different life periods.

In the first circle, I experience my love of nature, the land, and the ocean; the gifts from my mom and dad; the sailor and the farmer marrying. In the second circle, I experience meeting the people of this age, the culture, the society, the gift of both atheism and bland materialism. In the third circle, I see myself meeting my first medicine family, philosophy, and the arts. In the fourth circle, I am meeting education and choosing my way. In the fifth circle, I am in deep crisis and incarnating as me. In the sixth circle, I am learning to take responsibility, have a job, get married, have kids. In the seventh circle, I go through purgatory and meet the medicine. As I am standing in the middle of these circles, I hold myself and forgive and embrace all that has been. I am holding what needs to be held. I am releasing what needs to be released. I am forgiving myself and others. Then I start walking into the unknown. I feel the changes and the new challenge. I am sensing how medicine work becomes more active and present. I am opening my future. At fifty-nine—that is, in ten years' time—I am experiencing a big change. I see myself at seventy-seven; I meet the end. I see the period of reflection, and I see myself coming back. After all, this is the only place they serve coffee. This time we don't leave anyone behind; this time we all go. I know my destiny. I am holding the high dream. I am bringing hope. I am free.

Afterward, I take a long walk in Dyrehaven. After all, that is what I am. Free. To create my own life. Free to hold my ground. Free to dedicate my potential. In this walk, I sense acutely the changes that will occur from now and the next two life periods. In the deer park, I meet a flock of deer, in the middle a white one, flanked by two others. I see my root in this animal. I see my crown, but I also see that I am not alone. That my medicine family is with me.

THE RIVER OF MY SELF

I am pushing aside office life and administration. I know I need to embrace it instead of rejecting it. But it has been a long year. Like the guys doing the tarmac, I need a break. I flipped out during an institute meeting. The other heads of program agreed to eat my cake and have it. I went into my victim. I felt alone. I felt cheated. They need me, but they take my resources. I told them as much. Funny. To lose face completely, and behind this, knowing that I can trust my feelings. That at the end of the line, they also know they need me. Opening up actually made us look for a solution and find an alternative. So anger is not all bad, though it looks like it in the situation.

Going deep into my inner cave, I start listening to the river of my self. It is running slowly, trickling down the rocks in the dark. It is telling me that I actually managed. That I did a lot. But also that I spend too much. That I forget to care for my self. I let my sacred fire burn to the bottom before I refuel it. When I don't care for myself, I can't care for my nearest. It is telling me that I have a gift for setting others free, but that when I am not free myself, I can't help others. I need to free myself. I need to feel free in the situation. Not bound. Not obliged but free. Free to choose. Free to find my balance first. Free to regain my center when I lose it or am forced out of it. Free. In this I suddenly feel joy again. Trickling forth. Joy of life. That has been missing the last months with all the chores. Wauw. It's like a good friend. It's like color, sense, and smell all come back.

THIS IS THE ONLY PLACE
THEY SERVE COFFEE

Yesterday I was meditating and doing yoga by the harbor while StarEagle was doing her ballet class. It had been a couple of days, and I had been fooling around with my small I again, wondering what was inside that. Well, it came to me, the infinite embrace of this physical universe. Of the resistance, the nosebleed, the late hour at the office, the November morning in the rain. The smell of diesel, the sharp neon in the dissection room, the smell of carbolic soap in the terminal ward. The dust on the windowpane. The old road. The abandoned farm. The crowded street. The block of flats in the projects. The kids playing at dusk. The drunk down the corner. The ragman drawing circles. All of it. The friction lines. The weight. The meat. Down here in the well of gravity. The effort. The pulse. The rhythm. The web.

This is not how it is in the spirit world. We only get to stay here in this life a few winters. Then we return. Did we get what we came here for? Did we enjoy the sunrise or the sunset after a long day of hard labor, in the sweat of our faces? There is only one sunset that looks like that. When you finish work, and the day closes. It doesn't look like that for a molecule or an energy being. It only looks like that in the flesh. With blisters on your hands, with the smell of your energy spent on your skin, with the burden of outcome, good or bad, in your mind. This is the only place they serve coffee. This is the life world. The world made physical. So awaken the privilege of fulfillment and manifestation. Here in the flesh.

THE STAR CHILDREN

I am realizing my responsibility. That this year is about stepping into it. Stepping into responsiveness. Not reacting but taking responsibility for placing myself in situations where I react when I have lost my balance, when I have been forced out of my center. Regain balance. Find your center. Hold your ground. Remember that you are not alone.

Remember that you are at the center. Not lost, not wandering, but exactly where you should be. Take the time to be in-between. To come back to life. Make the space for yourself. Give to yourself before others. Stand for yourself.

Stand by giving light to yourself first. Nurturing your own spirit fire. Tending your sacred flame. Not moving when it is wavering. Not acting but responding, pausing, stopping to feel. To listen to the voice of my self. Making space.

Making time. Not running by the clock, not executing but sensing, being, feeling, standing.

As I am drawing a great spiral on a piece of paper, everything comes together. As a teacher taking care of the star children, remembering that I am limitless. That I came from the stars myself. Remembering coming out of the dreaming ceremony at Lalita in the early hours of morning, seeing Andromeda in the immense distance of the universe. Like driving past a house where you once lived in the dead of night. Trusting my nature. Being patient. Changing myself. Knowing that I am illuminating the path. Walking in beauty with Mother Nature. Questing for the sacred. Remembering the questing wheel. Asking. Listening. Claiming. Thanking. As one who returns. Finding my way through darkness, knowing this to be true, knowing this to be my gift, knowing this to be my path. As a medicine man and healer. As a writer. Holding the high dream. Peace in seven generations. As an artist and philosopher. Working for the Great-Grandmother. Building the pink cloud. Working for Mother Nature. Protecting the life force. Returning.

THE TRUE STORY

I walk in beauty,
And the beauty of Mother Earth
Walks in me.

I am bringing forth my light.
I illuminate the way.
Through me, the eternal light shines.

My heart flows over with love.
My energy is like the clear spring.
In my hands is healing.

I am the clear spring,
The eternal well, the sacred spring again.
I am dreaming the highest dream.

I think beautiful thoughts.
I say kind words.
I do beautiful deeds.

I see the potential in the problems,
The teaching in the challenges.
I see with kindness.

I see the love in the others.
Myself in what I don't like.
I am seeing with love.

I see my emotions as holy messengers.
I listen to my body,
Honoring it as the temple of my soul.

I hold myself.
I nurture my own sacred fire.

I let the others walk their own ways.

I make room for the human I am.
I remember who I am.
I choose love.

DISCLAIMER

Many people pay good money for a personal mantra. I have known some myself.

People, not mantras.

I only know one mantra.

This is the maha mantra, the great mantra, and it is free:

Hare Krishna, hare Krishna, Krishna, Krishna, hare, hare.
Hare Rama, hare Rama, Rama, Rama, Rama, Rama, hare, hare.

If it makes your life worse, come and get your money back.
If it makes your life better, I am not to be held responsible.

THREE BLIND MICE

Be transcendental to the three characteristics of the material universe: goodness, passion, and ignorance. Be free of any duality. Free yourself of the duality between good and bad. There exist no good or bad feelings. Only feelings exist, and they come and go. That is the truth of feelings, that they are temporal. Messengers. Free yourself of the duality between passion and neglect. After all, the Tao asks, "What is a good man but a bad man's teacher, and what is a bad man but a good man's job?" Free yourself of the duality between ignorance and evil. Love is the highest form of knowledge. True knowledge is eternal because it comes from reality, and reality comes from eternity. The truth is that your soul is eternal, and the reality that your body will die someday soon. Be situated in your original position, free of angst, free of desire. Be transcendent to material matters, and live in the spiritual universe already in this material contingent world. Enjoy eternally in complete knowledge and unconditional love.

MY METHOD IN FOUR MOVEMENTS

Jean Luc Godard said,
"If Cinema = Life then $1 + 2 + 3 = 4$."

I always thought that $1 + 2 = 3$.
That is what they told me at school.
But then I realized
Godard is just counting
Instead of adding.

The first, the second, and the third.
And then comes the fourth.

This is how I live my life.
I let things come to me instead of calculating.
That is why the Tao loves me.
That is why the women hold me dear,
And the men think me wise.

That is what I build my happiness around.
Innocent as a child, building castles in the sand.

NEW LEDGER

I have arrived at peace. For a moment. How do I hold on to this peace? How do I live peacefully and enjoyably in this age of confusion and unrest? Yesterday I was doing a dedication ceremony to potential. In this ceremony, I was going deep through my previous life. In this I saw that joining the architecture profession was the most logical and humorous choice for someone like me. In an age without religion, even without ideology, the order of architecture is the closest thing. Close to what? To becoming a monk? To feeling a purpose? To live in a community with shared values? Perhaps all of them at once. See, it was not a conscious choice, and sometimes I have lamented it because I saw it as the second-best choice between becoming a real artist and making money.

Well, architects don't really make money. And I did take another education to fulfill my artistic dreams.

Now it seems that the choice was the right one. When I am alone with my ceremony, my yoga, my diet, and my writing, I feel very much at peace. I feel restored. At ease. I look out, and I see a whole world coming of age. I hold great hope for this world. And I accept the fast pace of things bringing us from the atrocity of the forties and to the love-ins of the sixties. Turbulent, dynamic, zigzag, roller coaster. The yuppies and the grunge each eating their share of Mother Earth's birthday cake. The extreme development of technological knowledge, not yet countered by an ethical or aesthetical one. But there is real evidence that we can develop and grow.

Conscience is needed, ethics is needed, spirituality is needed, and solidarity is needed. But there is hope for a common future; there is hope for peace. I am this hope. Many are.

Perhaps the first step is to make peace with yourself. I am an endless and eternal soul. I have not been born; I will not be born. I am eternal, and therefore, I am real, and because I am real, I am true. This is what I want, to be a hollow bone. To clear and release all the lower register of emotion in order to contain love, friendship, benevolence, compassion, humor. To follow the Tao. To be at ease. To be relaxed. To let go of the senses and the ten thousand things appearing and disappearing. To open my vibration up, and let go of all that is contracting and tightening. Does this mean that I have to go and live in a monastery? Perhaps. Or it means that right now, my family, friends, and working life are giving me all the training I need in order to let go, in order to relax, in order to simply be. Every time I think I have it, I am in balance, they will test if it is really so. Is this really you holding your center? Is this really you taking the high ground?

But holding and taking sound so uptight. The hollow bone does not take or hold. It clears and releases. So I have to make time and space to do this instead of identifying with the problems, the emotions, the situations. All things must pass. As clouds on a blue sky. Emotions are not real, whether they are good or bad, so the Buddhists say. But my true position is to have eternal joy, complete knowledge, and unconditional love. So I have to be transcendent to the three qualities of materialism; goodness, passion, and ignorance. This is the answer of the yogi. They are endlessly enjoying. What is my answer? Are emotions unreal, or are they the fuel of the soul? Jesus had passion. He didn't live in a monastery. Nor did the Vaisnava of the above truth. So how do I become a hollow bone? By clearing out the lower registrar or all of them? I think by letting the lower registrar go so that the higher register remains. To ask forgiveness for all the lower thoughts, acts, and deeds I have done. To clear and release them.

My thoughts are circling around this question of how to remain at peace when the humdrum of everyday life returns. How can I remain centered when it all starts over again? Right now, my answer is to do morning pages, morning practice, yoga, eat vegetables, and refrain from sugar, coffee, alcohol, meat. To be clear. To clean up myself. But also to give to myself before others. I have understood this as the practice of standing, standing for yourself and, thereby, standing for the whole. To remain whole no matter what. Now this is challenged every day in the great dojo of so-called reality. I have to remember that I chose this teaching myself. But also asking to the nature of this reality: Is it temporary, or is it holy? I think it is both. As Bagvadghita states, this material nature is the energy of God as we are integral fragments of God also. So I might ask, "How can I celebrate the holiness of everyday life? How can I see my daily life with the family as both a training in clearing out lower emotions and as a holy chore to raise and be responsible for other beings? How can I see my work, which is both challenging, wonderful, and awful at the same time, as a teaching and as a holy chore?" The Bagvadghita says that I must devote my effort to God so that I am no longer working for myself, for the fruits of my work, or in order to do good. I am simply doing my task as a favor to God. The same goes for family life. Good or bad are material values. So rather than being a good or bad parent, it is about being a loving parent. It is about giving up achieving, giving up effort, perfection. Instead, it is about dedication, being, receiving. The pursuit of fruit-bearing activities will all fail in the end, whether it is good parenting or working for a cause. As long as I cling to these material values, I will not be free. I will not be unattached. I will not be undetermined. And when I am unfree, attached, and determined, being a good parent is impossible. Søren Kierkegaard said, "If I marry I will regret, If I don't marry I will also regret." Being attached to outcomes will make me uptight, and it will make me lose my temper. So I can learn to control my temper, but all my effort will now go into this. Instead, I must release my attachment to the outcome. To become a clear channel, open to what is, valuating what is, appreciating what is. Seeing the teaching and the holy nature of so-called reality. It is real because it is unendingly changing. It is true because it is ever teaching us. And it is holy because it prompts us to become whole.

Yesterday I was doing a deep ceremony of listening to the voice of underground river of my self. I sat in deep meditation, listening to the voice of my self tell me the story of how I became who I am in this lifetime. Of the seven times seven circles making up my forty-nine years, and how each circle has provided teaching, insight, skills, and knowledge through experience that was often hard. In this meditation, it became clear to me how deeply impacted I have been by my parents, their inner states, and their emotional instabilities. How I have integrated their lack of self-esteem, love for themselves, anger, and sadness. How these have been planted in my garden of consciousness and how I have cultivated them, believing them to be my own roots. There has been a lot of gardening and weeding to do to come to this understanding from my mentor, from my homeopat, from the medicine, and from my shamanic journey with Magic Moon Wolf. The simplicity of it. I am not this body. This body is part of nature. I am eternal, endless, undying, and on this spirit journey in this physical vessel in this determined and material world. To learn, to experience, to grow. But I am not these parents either. Their problems and their issues may have affected me, like a difficult math assignment with a trick answer, but my original state is different. I remember myself in the first circle of my life as joyous, humorous, innocent, loving, powerful, compassionate, friendly, laughing, and clear. This is my original position. This is very close to my spirit nature, as close as you can get in the flesh.

After doing this meditation, I went to the ocean again. And in the sweat lodge of the sauna, I saw something that I have been looking for: the portal of wisdom that Pythagoras said was at the end of the first seven life circles. As he holds it, we will develop ourselves through the challenges and teachings of life until we reach the age of forty-nine. At that age, we will either arrive at wisdom or stop development of our spiritual way. Perhaps this is so. I think there is still hope for those who don't. This is my own experience. However it may be, I have been looking for this with a mild expectancy. Yesterday it came to me in full force. That wisdom is to return to the innocence of childhood. Perhaps this is not for everyone, but for me, this holds a deep meaning. To return to my true nature of love, compassion, innocence, and joy. To let all the negative expectancies of experience go, to clear, to release, and to keep the gems of wisdom while being a happy fool. Happy as a fool, innocent as a child. I know the universe is looking after me. I know that Krishna is my friend. I am with the Great-Grandmother, the lion of Zion is in my heart, and I am guided by the knowledge of Mary and the forgiveness of the virgin mother. I am with Mother Earth, and Mother Earth is in me. I want to release all the old stuff—emotions, thoughts, feelings, trauma—and become what I originally was, full of joy, laughter, and love. I want to become a hollow bone so that the marriage between heaven and earth can be consumed and expressed through me. So that the light of eternity may shine through me, and the love of the great ones may be expressed through me and manifested in this life world.

This morning as I was relieving myself, a small fly came to bite me. I asked it not to, but it persisted. It imposed itself on me to take my blood even though I had not allowed it. So I caught it and placed underneath a plastic cup. There in the dark it wondered what had happened to it. As I finished my business, I removed the cup and asked it to be free. It sat still as a stone, perhaps expecting death, perhaps in bewilderment. I blessed it and gave it a sacred breath of life. At once it flew, a little drunk perhaps, but it ended up on the wall, where it balanced itself again and sat still. I wonder about this incident.

As it happened, I thought, *This is also my position. I have been imposing myself on God and he has placed me here in this dark universe to rethink my status.* I am thinking about the bad things I have done in my life, and it comes to me that the karma we produce in life is connected to the karma that brought us into this material world in the first place. I am not sure why I am here. One part of me tells me that I came here in order to bring hope. That I am a star child, and I am illuminating the way for the other star children born in this age. This is so. Another part tells me that Krishna and I are great friends, and he has placed me here in order to regain humbleness, soberness, and respect. Perhaps both are true. He is a great friend in my heart, and I take him to be the father of the Christ. But the other thing is also true. Like the arc of the birds flight and the instantaneous swing of its wing are both true. This is the only place they serve coffee, and I have fallen in love with this planet. And even though I am not a real Vaisnava, a declared devotee, I hold pity for the fallen ones who do not see that they are not determined or conditioned by this universe.

As I am writing this, I am engaged with passion and the hara chakra. How can I create balance there, where desire and lust reside now instead of pleasure? Desire is unsatisfiable, and once satisfied it turns to ashes. This is not true pleasure. This is suffering. Ask one who knows. I was drinking every day for many years, drinking to keep away the pain and to return to pleasure only to find more suffering as the haze lifted. So what is this unbalance? I have not become religious. My consideration about the fly in the cup is for this. This unbalance brought me here. So what is needed to find this balance again? My inner heart tells me it is a choice I have to make. A decision. So I make this decision. It can take many forms; right now it has the form of women. I look at them, and I think sexual thoughts. This is stupid. I would never realize those thoughts. I do not want the women to receive these thoughts. Don't do this. Instead, appreciate their beauty. Realize that it does not belong to them. It is the beauty of nature. Do not release your sexual energy.

Instead, lift it to your heart, and when you and your woman consummate your relationship, let it be an act of love made physical. Lift the energy of the two snakes to the center of your head, and refill the sacred chalice. Then let all your energy into your KA body, your energy body, your energy field. Continue to do this until you are nothing but light.

THE STORY OF MYSELF
IN SEVEN STEPS

I sit down in a deep meditation to listen to my higher self. The underground river of myself. The true voice of who I am. In this meditation I am told the following story.

Once upon a time, there was a little boy. He loved the trees. He loved the flowers. And he loved the animals. He lived in a beautiful forest in a beautiful house. He loved his mom, and he loved his dad. They would go on expeditions with his two brothers, and all of them would explore and cherish the world. They would go to the beautiful ocean and the cliffs. They would go to the countryside to stay at a farm with animals. The sun would be shining, and everything would be beautiful. The little boy was full of joy, laughter, love, compassion, and spirit. He read stories for his friends from leaves he found on the bushes. He picked flowers for his mom and sat by the curb until his dad came home. He talked to the trees and laughed with the sun.

Then the little boy noticed that his mom and dad had problems. His mom was feeling bad, and his dad was sad. Sometimes his dad got angry. The little boy tried to help his parents, but they just felt worse and became sadder and angrier. The little boy thought that it had something to do with him, so he felt guilty. He felt that he was the product of sad, bad, and angry, and that perhaps he was all of them at once. So he started to experiment with them. It's not that anything beautiful or nice didn't happen in this period. Let's just say that the negative experiences filled up most of the sky.

Then the little boy grew up and rebelled against this atmosphere of negativity and neglect. He threw everything overboard and jumped into life with all his force, all his appetite, and all his vitality. Again, everything was new and everything was great and every afternoon lasted forever. But somehow bad, sad, and angry were now part of this creation. The little boy who was now a young man also felt bad, sad, and angry and did negative deeds. Morals, he thought, were only for ordinary people. But bright young people like him would shine through history like there was no tomorrow.

Well, there was.

Waking up as an almost grown-up, our young man felt alone. He was alone. The party was over. He wanted to find a girlfriend. He wanted to find out what to do with his life. One day he was with his friends and heard them speaking about architecture school. He realized that he also wanted to do this. He had thought that he was a painter, but during the wild days, the bad vibes had sort of undermined his creative confidence. So he applied for school, a place that readily mixed rigid rules with open anarchy, that mixed poetry and softness with the rigors of military order. He also found a girlfriend. When she was feeling bad, things were good, but when she started to feel good, things got bad.

Then our hero rebelled again. Against school, against society, against growing up. He threw everything overboard in order to become an artist with two musicians. He even got accepted to a real art school, a school he had never dared to apply to when he was young. He reveled, he rocked, and he did good work. He even rebelled against his girlfriend, who had become a real pain in the ass. Then the house of cards fell together.

He eventually got help from his ex-girlfriend's therapist. Oh, yes. He learned how to get a job, how to get married, and how to start a family. He learned to help his mom and dad with their issues. He learned how to do a job interview. Then he got a job. He married his girlfriend. He got his first son. He also did his first movie. He wrote his first book. He had his second son. And all was well. Until one day it was over.

They had to move to a new house. Their old adviser had told them not to buy the place where they stayed. So they moved. Our now middle-aged man had accounts to settle. With self-medication—coffee, alcohol, and cigarettes. So he waged war against these in order to know his real feelings, in order not to feel he was living in a haze, in order to set his children free of this pattern. But as Jesus tell us in the Good Book, take care when you clean out your house of one demon. It will walk aimlessly around until it finds friends. They return to find the house nice and clean, and all the demons move in. The war lasted seven years. It had many victims—his good humor, his temper, his dignity, even his health. It almost cost him his marriage, his family, work, and life. But he won. In the end, he won. It was over, and he woke up as a patient who faced death but returned to the living.

Now he saw that he was no longer responsible for the feelings and actions of his mom and dad. Now he saw how their feelings had been woven into his life, his character, his actions. He saw what had been planted in his garden of consciousness, and he weeded out what wasn't his—anger, neglect, abuse, negativity, shame, guilt, felling small, unworthy, bad. All of this he weeded because he saw that it wasn't him. He was like he always had been—full of joy, loving, curious, adventurous, brave, unattached, undetermined, compassionate, humorous, sparkling, eternal as the spring, frivolous as Hera, clear as a mountain spring.

In the evening, I—the little boy of that story—drove to the ocean and meditated. It came to me that true wisdom is obtained at the end of the seventh circle by becoming a child again. As Panos used to say, a happy idiot. A fool. Innocent as a child. This is the true wisdom of the seventh circle.

I AM THE TASTE OF WATER

I am the color of fire.
I am the beauty of women.
I am the self-discipline of all ascetics.

DEEPENING LODGE

As this week alone draws to an end, I am collecting my experience and beginning to brace myself against returning to social life. There have been many deep experiences during the different ceremonies and meditations I have made.

One of the gems has been going through my seven life circles again. To see how the emotions of my mother and father blended with my own energy, creating new patterns of rejections and repeating old ones. I see myself as both the weaver and the woven one. The new deck of cards with the old rules. The dreamer and the dream.

My deep realization of wisdom is that I can return to source. Weed my garden of consciousness, write my own rules. And why is this possible? Because I have all the gems, all the teaching, all the experience of this intertwining with the energy of my parents. Now I need to let go of the guilt, the blame, the shame, and all the trauma connected with gaining this knowledge. But I know how to do that as well. How? Because I had to teach myself everything in order to survive. My parents and my society left me as a blank page, and I had to seek the wisdom in many places in order to survive, in order to become myself. I say this in a pragmatic kind of loving way. In fact, I have become quite fond of my Marxist-Lutheran upbringing, with its rational and materialistic approach.

I embrace this deep teaching. Thank you, my teachers. So I am ready to return to the source of the self with all these gems and all this knowing. From there, I will hopefully be able to help others caught in the same web, lighting the road ahead. I will return to the source of innocence, love, joy, friendship, and kindness. I will go to the Sundance, and I will dance for this.

I will dance for the tree and the children.
I will dance for innocence and joy.
I will dance for Mother Earth,
For love and for hope.

In this way, I anchor my stepping into wisdom. Happy as a child, innocent and joyful, with kindness as my religion, strength and wisdom on my brow, and healing in my hands and heart.

DISCIPLE OF THE SELF

As I am journeying in my car to the Sundance, I am going through all the podcasts WindEagle gave us so far. The creation intelligence, being a creator in this lifeworld. The perceptual intelligence, being with the world and entering the mystery through silence. The emotional intelligence, seeing that wholeness is only reached through the diversity of difference, pure difference. The pathfinding intelligence illuminating the way, walking in beauty. Sustaining intelligence, nurturing what is, healing what has been broken. In the car, the thought of my brothers and the conflict I have with them keeps occurring. I realize in utmost simplicity that I only have to forgive myself in order to change the energy of that system. When I have forgiven myself, I can speak my mind without hurting others.

In camp, everything is wet. It is raining cats and dogs. I find a nice place to camp, sheltered from the wind by an oak tree. I have been preparing for this dance, but I am restless and fidgety. Of course it will come, the clarity, the deepening. In the morning, I find a small altar in the woods. I bury my weapons there. Stringing our beads in society, one of the members share that she has been an abuser and is with the AA. We talk a lot about self-discipline, about being a disciple of the self. I realize that I went through the same. On my own. My own Golgatha. I perceive the energy of this Sundance. How deep and healing it is. How thorough. How penetrating. How forgiving. How merciless. Without compromise. Good old no surrender. It is pure love.

SOCIETY

As the days go by, things get busy at Sundance. We are building a lodge, running a camp, and preparing for a deep ceremony. Well, we are already in deep ceremony. The lunch society I am with continues running smoothly pointed by Moon Raven, a medicine woman running for MP. Great. Siegfried is also on board. Good old Siegfried already has a medicine name since Siegfried means the victorious peace. And he is. Victorious. I am getting along with these people, and we are producing a wonderful lunch for everyone who is working so hard.

In my other society, things are a bit different. The healer lodge society, co-pointed by Eagle Heart and Magic Moon Wolf, is a gathering of very diverse temperaments. I have been called in as understudy, youngest healer on the team. Swan Warrior, a former rugby and soccer star turned healer, and Singing Earth, Steiner teacher and Mensendich therapist, are also on the team. Then along comes the dark horse, Anders, a former karate champion and physiotherapist for the national basketball team. He starts out by fixing Magic Moon Wolf, who has a strained knee; Swan Warrior, who has several parting gifts from his rugby past; and me, who accidentally hurt my left toe. Okay, I am the new boy in class. All the others have experience, they know anatomy, they have clients, they get paid to do this. Uh oh. Do I really have the skills to be on this bill? Then the chief calls us in to see if we have our acts together. I look at my hands. They are what I am bringing. They are all I have to offer. No exams, no client base, no former experience.

OBSTACLES

"That toe is broken," Anders tell me as he tapes me up for the community round. "A broken toe is not enough to keep you off the court." Okay, I dance the community round, and we have agreed to look things over the next morning. "You won't be dancing more rounds than once a day," Anders tells me. The toe is doing good, the circulation is healing and beneficial, but there is a golden measure here, and it isn't five rounds a day. It's one. One. So what do you do when you have been preparing for the Sundance, actually figured out how to distribute the kids so you could go alone, and then find out that you can't dance? What's good about this? What's the added value here?

Well, I can pray. I am all three and thirteen. I live in number 13, for God's sake. I don't think I make much of this, but that's one thing I can do. Pray. I have prepared, and I know what I am praying for. So I take the kachina of a broken toe as a gift. I get up at seven. Pray for three rounds. Then I go fix lunch. Come back to the wheel at two. Anders tapes me up so I can dance my daily round. High noon, when the going gets tough on the dancers out there in the sun. Pray another three rounds and help Magic Moon Wolf in the healing lodge between dances. Then eat dinner and back for the closing round at eight. This is actually working. It's more than that. It is a gift. It makes me go deep. I sit with the cormorant medicine, going deep.

HONORING SONG

I have chosen to go to this Sundance alone since it is my third, and third is West. Time to go deep. Time to sink into myself. Time to look into myself. Spend time with myself. Do something for me before others. So I let the kids stay at home. I rejected having other dancers with me on my ride. I came to the dance alone. I live alone, between the trees in a little outside camp. The only thing I didn't turn down was the duty in the healing lodge. I needed to step up for that. I saw that in my destiny walk and drawing the spiral drawing with the life circles in the Southwest.

So I am sitting in deep meditation, and gradually, this kachina becomes clear to me. Yes, I need to go deep. I have to sit for all the rounds when I am not on call and pray. Pray for innocence and joy. Pray for the tree and the children. Pray for Mother Earth. Pray for love. Pray for hope. It comes to me in one of the rounds. Second cycle. Second dance. Mother Earth. I have to see my woman and my kids as the nearest representation of Mother Earth in my life. I have to honor this. I have to honor them. And deeper yet. I have to honor and protect the sacred feminine in myself. This is why I hurt my foot, my heart tells me. What does this mean? How do I do that?

THE WORD BECOME FLESH

Sitting for many rounds, my head becomes heavy. It's what I am dreading. Headaches. Had them since childhood. Splitting. I am wondering if there is any aspirin in camp. It's my weak point. When I woke up with hangovers in the old days, I would just start off with another round, trying to avoid the pain. Now I embrace that. And the pain. I sit in it. I release; I let it go. I give it to Mother Earth. Then I open myself. The dancers are nearing trance. Some seem to be punch-drunk by now, others in pain. There are only four dancers out there now since one of them has gone to take a crap in the forest, and another one had to drop out. There is only one chief in the lodge, too, since one is drumming, and one is away. It seems we are a long way from home here. I open myself. I allow for their pain to be transferred to me as a hollow bone. I am asking for their pain to be delivered to my address. I let it go. My head is swirling with pain. I sink it. I release it. I am a hollow bone now. I receive the pain, and I let it through my channel right down to the Earth Mother. I release. After each round, I go to a place in the forest. There I clear out everything that is still clinging to me.

A theme has merged with my preparation prayer. To walk the beauty way, I must first weed my garden of consciousness. In order to think beautiful thoughts, speak beautiful words, do beautiful deeds, I must learn to be responsible for what I think, what I do, what I say. To understand that what I eat, read, watch has a bearing on how I will think, talk, and act. What I think isn't neutral either. Those thoughts become words, and those words become actions. The word become flesh. So to get out of reactive behavior, I must become responsible in order to respond. Responsible. For my thoughts. My thoughts. My responsibility. Each little one of them. Mine. Like a weed. In a garden. I am dancing for this. I am praying for this. To become the gardener.

THE COLLECTIVE GARDEN
OF CONSCIOUSNESS

In the purification lodge, the lion comes back to me. This time it is really heavy. It's like a small sun. A big lion with a corona of flame. I am roaring. I am letting go. In the womb. This is not an avatar or a power animal. This is me. The lodge is filled with energy. Anders is there. Magic Moon Wolf. Siegfried. The warriors. Like me, we are going deep. They are with me. I am allowing the transformation. Red Heart Coyote asks us to conclude. Words, they can mean the world. I chose not to say anything, and I feel a fraud. In the dark I had the courage to roar like a lion, but I don't have the guts to claim it when I am asked to speak up. As we are exiting, there is my second chance. Spirit always gives you a second chance. People are howling as they leave the lodge one by one. I make a roar as I come out and say, "I am the lion."

In the healing lodge, we have gotten our act together. We have put up our small pavilion and decorated it with flowers in the colors of the eight directions. We are going on a shamans' walk, the five of us, single-file. We pass the tree that Hans, the master of the forest, saved after the great storm in '81. He pulled it up with his tractor, and it is still alive but standing slanted over the road, like the Tower of Pisa. I ask it how it's doing, and it says, "Great. Thanks. What doesn't kill you makes you stronger." "Mmmhh," I reply, "but you are still kinda skewed. That can't be healthy." "Huh," the tree replies, "There are thousands and thousands of trees in these here woods, but apart from the little one you are all dancing around, tell me what trees other than me do you know and speak about?" The tree has humor. It comes from great trials, I guess. As we are doing a sharing round on this walk, a thought comes to me. It is not enough that I weed my garden of consciousness. We as humankind must also weed our collective gardens of consciousness. I open this theme in the healer's circle. I am praying for this. So are they.

NAMING DAY

In my medicine book I have drawn the image of the lion with the corona. This drawing has a name: Lion Heart. *Løvehjerte* in Danish. This is an unexpected crisis. I didn't wanna change my name. Clear Spring is a great name. It is the name of my energy self. It's not something I am growing out of. When I am in the healing lodge, I work intuitively, sensing the chakras and energy bodies of the dancers coming in. I don't think, and it wouldn't help me if I did because I have no formal training. I just do. That is Clear Spring. That's energy working through my hands, telling them what to do. Seeing through my eyes, telling them what to notice. How can I discard that name for another? It's the broom of the lady. *Escobar de la mujer.* It's not something to throw away lightly.

I am consulting WindEagle. As always, things are simple with her. "You can have two names," she tells me. I feel the truth in these words. Clear Spring needs a name to shield her. That's is how I feel. That this is the inner wedding consumed. The two names are holding each other. They are working together. They are one, meaning the same. But from each their perspective. In my medicine book, I make a drawing. Clear Spring and Lion Heart walking in the garden of collective consciousness. That's how I see it. Lion Heart is needed to continue our work with weeding the collective garden of consciousness, as we did in the Cherish project in the Marble Church. Well perhaps I do have a little track record after all. Only one former client, but a big one. I smile as I make for the healing lodge. This will be all right. My hands are laughing.

THIS BEING IS ME

In the final stringing after the dance, I get up and claim my name. It's not a new name, but it is a formal name. It's the lion and the lamb. I am nervous. But I have been dancing the last round on this. I have been to the woods, talking and rehearsing my speech with some of my plant friends and the trees. As I was dancing yesterday, a great kite showed itself above the box where the chiefs are sitting. I looked up the kite in my animal spirit guide. It stated calmly, "Take off your mask." So I am, claiming this name, Lion Heart. I will walk in the garden of collective consciousness with it.

In the car on my way home, I don't even stop for gas. I am alone. I am not thinking. Not a single thought. I am finding my still point, resting in the quiet. How wonderful that is. I don't speak, I don't think, I don't eat. I am just there. Driving. Being. In a being state of pure being. I feel all the energies and all the love of the people I have just parted with almost as a perfume enwrapping me. I am just here. If a thought occurs, I don't even register. If a need arises, I know it is not real. I don't need to stop for a hamburger. In fact, I don't eat meat. I am just here. Right now. And I love it. I am in the West. Deeply emerged in this world, in the physical universe, in this universal body, just being, just traveling through space and time in this galaxy, in this cosmology. My core is this being. This being is me. It's not the other way around—that I am this being, or my ego owns this body. No way, José. The fact is this being state is me. This being is me. The state of pure being.

ACKNOWLEDGMENTS

Many of the insights and much of the knowledge shown here were taught to me by WindEagle Kinney Litton as part of my training as an evocative leader with the EHAMA Institute. The basic assumption being that in this time and age, we are the peoples of the corn, returning from the four directions to share our gems and learnings.

I have freely shared what I was given to see of the red path by WindEagle and the teachings of the Delicate Lodge, while sharing my own findings from the other paths. I want to extend my gratitude to her and to Red Heart Coyote, Ancient Starchild, Singing the Sun, and Diamond Panther, as well of my circle, the Ripplemakers, for holding me in these teachings. I also honor the circle of the people's European Sundance. Alongside these teachings, I have been taught by Magic Moon Wolf, and some of her guiding and teaching is manifested here. The idea to collect this experience came to me from the South African healer and medicine woman Teya K. Estar.

I also want to credit the path of science, the white road, as I have been raised in and where I hold numerous degrees as a master, a teacher, an artist, and a scientist. My acknowledgment and thanks go out to those who helped and solicited my way here, among them Kjeld Vindum, Arne Bro, Anne Wivel, Cort Dinesen, Peter Henning Jørgensen, Anders Michelsen, Henrik Oxvig, and my mentor of philosophy Panos Charbis. First and foremost to my mother, the first doctorate being I met in this lifeworld and whose love of language and structural thinking carries me through life.

To my brothers for sharing the experience of growing up in a western society, to my mother for showing me the love of ocean and to my father for showing me nature, the pasture and the woods. To the trees for helping to raise me.

The yellow road, where I have trained and done much unsupervised study, was founded in my practice of Tai-chi Yuan taught to me by Malthe Blegvad. Thank you. And from the unparalleled insight of the translation of the Tao de Ching by Stephen Mitchell.

For the black tradition, I am thankful not least to my family, who show me that the blending of the corn is not just a mental exercise but a physical reality. This book is dedicated to my wife and partner in changing the energy structure of this planet, Veronica S. Hodges, and our children—Morgan, Elias, and Vega—as the corn already blended.

Ingram Content Group UK Ltd.
Milton Keynes UK
UKHW012237170423
420333UK00012B/424/J

9 781480 889538